Defining a BETTER Way to Operate

Can You Survive the Age of Disruption?

Creating the All-in Culture

RESOURCE GUIDE

The Best

JK Buller
4/17

JOHN K. BULLER
Loyalty Solutions Group

Compliments of

 ARISTA POINT

Improving the Employee Benefit Experience
www.AristaPoint.com

THE
**LOYALTY SOLUTIONS
GROUP**
Cultures Built On Continuous Feedback

Defining a better way to operate.

First Printing: September 2016
ISBN-10 0-9979952-0-3 **paperback**
ISBN-13 978-0-9979952-0-6 **paperback**

Library of Congress Catalog Number:
2016952716

Loyalty Solutions Group
jkbuller@loyaltysolutionsgroup.com
Seattle, WA, 98109
www.loyaltysolutionsgroup.com

Ordering Information: Quantity sales.
*Special discounts are available on quantity purchases by
corporations, associations, and others. For details, contact Loyalty
Solutions Group at **jkbuller@loyaltysolutionsgroup.com**.
For orders by trade bookstores and wholesalers, please contact
Loyalty Solutions Group.*

First Edition
10 9 8 7 6 5 4 3 2 1

THE LOYALTY SOLUTIONS GROUP
Cultures Built On Continuous Feedback

Management Seminar, Coaching and Consulting

To: "Surviving over 40 years of Senior Management"

HOW TO USE THIS RESOURCE GUIDE

There are four elements to creating an ALL-IN Culture:

- All stakeholders share a relentless ALL-IN to accomplish the organization's mission and desired outcomes.

- All organizational stakeholders are ALL-IN owning and adhering the organizational process and protocols.

- All organizational stakeholders are ALL-IN understanding the individual leadership and management behaviors that are the foundation for collaborative/innovative cultures.

- All organizational stakeholders are ALL-IN trusting organizational decision competency.

Getting to a new and embraced ALL-IN Culture will take all of the skills required with any organizational change.

Organizational leaders today are tasked with an almost impossible amount of required intelligences.

Today's leadership needs to be proficient in understanding the **Myers-Briggs Profile** – knowing yourself and understanding others – which was the intelligence lesson of the 1980s and early '90s. Then along came **emotional intelligence**, which focused on street-smarts vs. book-smarts.

Over the last 10 years, leaders have also needed to be competent in understanding the social media explosion, or social media intelligence.

It also helps if you have **ethnic intelligence, religious intelligence,** and **immigration intelligence.** And now, the biggest new understanding is **generational intelligence.**

This resource guide is not designed to be read as a book, unless you want to explore the full spectrum of cultural processes that comprise the defining elements of a culture. It is meant to address specific topics that may be challenging to your current state of affairs.

The sections are designed to help you gain insight into how you might take better advantage of the process.

ALWAYS TRY TO MAKE YOUR CULTURE BETTER

. . .READ WHEN NEEDED.

Table of Contents

Curiosity:
The Fuel for Passion;
the Antidote for Fear.

There has always been a discussion about what drives people to excel in what they do, or find the secret to something new. What is it about the human experience that keeps some people self-motivated and driven, while others seem to never have the energy to extend their worlds?

"What makes people curious? Is it something that you were born with?"

I believe that a person's level of curiosity, and conscious understanding of the emotions and behaviors of that curiosity, is the answer to this human dilemma. Curiosity truly is the fuel for an individual's passion, and the antidote for an individual's fears.

Passion and fear are the two most powerful human drivers of behaviors. Think about the most productive, interesting, and, may I say, fun people you know. What makes them different?

Think about those friends of yours who always seem tired and just too busy to get everything done, even though you can't understand what they are doing.

I believe the core difference between these two kinds of friends is the level of curiosity that they have or don't have.

So this begs the question: What makes people curious? Is it something that you were born with? Can someone be taught to be curious? Can someone just suddenly get curious?

What about the impact of an individual being curious, and the idea that an organization as a whole can be curious?

What is the impact of having individuals who are not curious in the organizational culture?

"The power of curiosity is wanting to know and understand what was said."

I believe that hiring people who are naturally curious is a secret formula that will have significant impact on the overall organizational culture. At the same time, I believe that you can impact a culture by creating an environment that enables individuals to discover their own curiosity, which can and will have a significant positive impact on all parts of the organization.

Let's talk about the behaviors that enable individuals to discover their curiosity. Let's start with your own curiosity

level – how do you know when you are curious about something? What is the first emotion/feeling you notice?

It starts with you wanting to know about something that you are not sure about.

In my case, it is usually me wanting to know the definition of the word or concept topic. When I hear a concept or word that someone uses, by nature I want to get a definition so I understand what was just talked about.

This curious activity happens to be the outcome of me working very hard at listening with the intent to understand what someone is saying.

This is my #1 preferred behavior for any culture – always make sure you clarify and understand what others are saying.

Curiosity is driven by the behavior of trying to understand something that was said or presented – not just letting it go by.

The second driver in my curiosity is wanting to understand the impact that this new thought or concept might have on outcomes that I have been challenged to manage or support.

It is driven by a level of commitment to be successful. This is also a core tenant of the ALL-IN Culture – being very committed to the mission and the desired outcomes, for the organization, or your family.

The power of curiosity is wanting to know and understand what was said – with the idea that you are committed to being successful in accomplishing a desired outcome.

The ability to create a curious organizational culture is the foundation of an ALL-IN Culture.

People being ALL-IN for the desired outcomes of the mission.

People being driven to understand what people are saying and wanting to understand the potential impact that the thought or concepts might have.

People having faith in the decision processes and protocols, making it easy to support agreed upon initiatives for change.

And finally, decisions being made with a total group commitment to being successful.

The second element of curiosity is the power it has in confronting fear. Fear is the most forceful human factor. Fear usually causes people to freeze, as they are confronted with the hopelessness of the outcome – and unable

to visualize anything except the worst possible outcome.

I would suggest that this paradigm has changed for those that have been diagnosed with cancer. Twenty years ago, cancer was viewed as a death sentence. In today's world, with increased treatment options and technologies, people with cancer diagnoses are challenged to get curious and act with hope – to seek out ways to live through it: "What are the options? How can I change to raise my chances of beating the disease?"

Cancer survivors talk about how that experience changed their entire lives. This new will toward curiosity extends into all aspects of their lives, because they've had to engage – and keep going through the fear. Curiosity becomes the energy that is at the root of fighting the disease.

In organizations, this sense of fear comes when business turns south – and the organization is confronted with the reality of adapt or die.

Again, one of two things might happen: The organization's culture falls into disarray or the culture uses its skills in managing curiosity, to allow it to fight for a way to adapt to the new situation.

Curiosity is defined as a strong desire to know or learn something.

Which kind of person or organization would you like to be?

I suggest that you...

Stay CURIOUS, my friends.

Creating the ALL-IN Culture

There are four elements to creating an ALL-IN Culture:

- All stakeholders share a relentless ALL-IN to accomplish the organization's mission and desired outcomes
- All stakeholders are ALL-IN owning and adhering to the organizational process and protocols
- All stakeholders are ALL-IN understanding the individual leadership and management behaviors that are the foundation for collaborative/ innovative cultures
- All stakeholders are ALL-IN trusting organizational decision competency

ALL-IN CULTURE

This is an attempt to blend the needed elements of the traditional command and

control culture that the Baby Boomers are attached to, with the elements of the growing trend of people defining their chosen lifestyle, and prioritizing lifestyle over being successful – as measured by the amount of money and toys collected.

When you look at the factors that define command and control culture, it is obvious that no one wins. The All-IN Culture redefines the system that everyone has to agree upon, to get what the organization requires in order to manage the constant change in our current business environment.

HOW DO WE GET THERE?

Getting to a new and embraced ALL-IN Culture will take all of the skills required with any organizational change. Organizational leaders today are tasked with an almost impossible amount of required intelligences. Today's leadership needs to be proficient in understanding the Myers-Briggs Profile – knowing yourself and understanding others was the intelligence lesson of the 1980s and early '90s Then along came emotional intelligence, which focused on street smarts vs. book smarts.

Over the last 10 years, leaders have needed to be competent in understanding the social media explosion. It also helps if you have ethnic intelligence, religious intelligence, and immigration intelligence. And now, the biggest new understanding is generational intelligence.

The ability to have empathy for all of the above Intelligences, and the skill to manage culture change, concurrent with competency in driving your business model, seems like a large and daunting task. I contend that all these factors in the mix at the same time may make this ALL-IN Culture shift easier than in previous times.

Complexity forces simplicity.

WHY I'M INTERESTED IN BUILDING PRODUCTIVE CULTURES

I became interested in the concept of culture and leadership while I was at the University of Washington. As a college basketball player, how do you get 12 young men to understand the coach's system and play their role in helping the team be successful?

I was blessed to get two extra years of university education, earning my MBA while acting as the graduate assistant basketball coach. When it came time to write my thesis, I decided to focus on what then was called "Theory X vs. Theory Y" or democratic vs. autocratic leadership developed by Douglas McGregor in his 1960 book entitled, *The Human Side of Enterprise.*

Theory X was the thought that employees needed to be closely supervised under a comprehensive system of behavioral control.

Theory Y suggested that employees can learn to seek out and accept responsibility, and to exercise self-control and self-direction in accomplishing organizational objectives.

I contrasted the coaching styles of two great college coaches, Marv Harshman and Tex Winter, both Hall of Fame coaches. Coach Harshman was a coach that tailored his system to match his talent [Theory Y], while Coach Winter only allowed the players to work within his system [Theory X].

WHICH DO YOU BELIEVE TO BE THE BE THE MOST PRODUCTIVE WAY TO WIN BASKETBALL GAMES?

I discovered that both styles could be very successful. The real issue was getting the players to be ALL-IN with the coach's system and to be accountable for playing their role within that system.

Over the last 40 years of being a manager of people I have found the same to be true for regular business and government employees.

To be successful at accomplishing almost anything with a group of individuals, the most important thing that leadership can do is to make sure that everyone involved is: **ALL-IN** on the four basic factors of an ALL-IN organizational culture.

- **ALL-IN** to accomplish the organization's mission and desired outcomes
- **ALL-IN** owning and adhering o the organizational process and protocols
- ALL-IN understanding the individual leadership and management behaviors that are the foundation for a collaborative/innovative culture
- ALL-IN trusting organizational decision competency.

There is a second question that needs to be understood:

WHICH WOULD YOU RATHER HAVE?

A GREAT ORGANIZATIONAL CULTURE

-or-

A GREAT ORGANIZATIONAL STRATEGY

The last time Human Resources [Personnel] departments played a major role in an organization's business strategy was in the early 1980s, when the country added customer service as a required business strategy element. The book, *The Nordstrom Way*, written by Robert Spector, was – and is still – one of the leading voices

control culture that the Baby Boomers are attached to, with the elements of the growing trend of people defining their chosen lifestyle, and prioritizing lifestyle over being successful – as measured by the amount of money and toys collected.

When you look at the factors that define command and control culture, it is obvious that no one wins. The All-IN Culture redefines the system that everyone has to agree upon, to get what the organization requires in order to manage the constant change in our current business environment.

HOW DO WE GET THERE?

Getting to a new and embraced ALL-IN Culture will take all of the skills required with any organizational change. Organizational leaders today are tasked with an almost impossible amount of required intelligences. Today's leadership needs to be proficient in understanding the Myers-Briggs Profile – knowing yourself and understanding others was the intelligence lesson of the 1980s and early '90s Then along came emotional intelligence, which focused on street smarts vs. book smarts.

Over the last 10 years, leaders have needed to be competent in understanding the social media explosion. It also helps if you have ethnic intelligence, religious intelligence, and immigration intelligence. And now, the biggest new understanding is generational intelligence.

The ability to have empathy for all of the above Intelligences, and the skill to manage culture change, concurrent with competency in driving your business model, seems like a large and daunting task. I contend that all these factors in the mix at the same time may make this ALL-IN Culture shift easier than in previous times.

Complexity forces simplicity.

WHY I'M INTERESTED IN BUILDING PRODUCTIVE CULTURES

I became interested in the concept of culture and leadership while I was at the University of Washington. As a college basketball player, how do you get 12 young men to understand the coach's system and play their role in helping the team be successful?

I was blessed to get two extra years of university education, earning my MBA while acting as the graduate assistant basketball coach. When it came time to write my thesis, I decided to focus on what then was called "Theory X vs. Theory Y" or democratic vs. autocratic leadership developed by Douglas McGregor in his 1960 book entitled, *The Human Side of Enterprise*.

Theory X was the thought that employees needed to be closely supervised under a comprehensive system of behavioral control.

Theory Y suggested that employees can learn to seek out and accept responsibility, and to exercise self-control and self-direction in accomplishing organizational objectives.

I contrasted the coaching styles of two great college coaches, Marv Harshman and Tex Winter, both Hall of Fame coaches. Coach Harshman was a coach that tailored his system to match his talent [Theory Y], while Coach Winter only allowed the players to work within his system [Theory X].

WHICH DO YOU BELIEVE TO BE THE BE THE MOST PRODUCTIVE WAY TO WIN BASKETBALL GAMES?

I discovered that both styles could be very successful. The real issue was getting the players to be ALL-IN with the coach's system and to be accountable for playing their role within that system.

Over the last 40 years of being a manager of people I have found the same to be true for regular business and government employees.

To be successful at accomplishing almost anything with a group of individuals, the most important thing that leadership can do is to make sure that everyone involved is: **ALL-IN** on the four basic factors of an ALL-IN organizational culture.

- **ALL-IN** to accomplish the organization's mission and desired outcomes
- **ALL-IN** owning and adhering o the organizational process and protocols
- ALL-IN understanding the individual leadership and management behaviors that are the foundation for a collaborative/innovative culture
- ALL-IN trusting organizational decision competency.

There is a second question that needs to be understood:

WHICH WOULD YOU RATHER HAVE?

A GREAT ORGANIZATIONAL CULTURE

-or-

A GREAT ORGANIZATIONAL STRATEGY

The last time Human Resources [Personnel] departments played a major role in an organization's business strategy was in the early 1980s, when the country added customer service as a required business strategy element. The book, *The Nordstrom Way*, written by Robert Spector, was – and is still – one of the leading voices

on the discussion of customer service in America.

Since the early 2000s, businesses began shifting their focus to continuous improvement, which has been mainly about cutting expenses. The goal was to improve profitability by doing everything possible to lower costs. In most cases, this meant having less people doing more work at as a low a wage as possible.

As is always the case, this business strategy can only be sustained so long before a host of outside influences take over. People can only be pushed so far and at some point this focus on What we do and How we do it better, creates a disconnect between the employees and their passion for doing their jobs.

This is the first time in history that there are three different generations working in the economy: Baby Boomers, Generation-Xers, and the Millennials. The Millennials need to work as they play – socially and collaboratively. Command and control culture does not work with this group, and "loyalty" and "waiting your turn" are "total loser" concepts with Millennials.

Over the last couple of years, as the business climate has gotten better, a new dilemma has appeared. New opportunities and new products are now the new norm. You either innovate or you look at the distinct possibility that your business will fail.

This dilemma has accelerated the discussion about which organizational culture enables the most innovation.

The answer to this question: Culture executes a strategy, strategy does not create a culture.

Conclusion:

There is no secret sauce that someone can buy to create an ALL-IN Culture. These cultures are built on having people ALL-IN on the basic human interactions that can be taught and learned by all levels of an organization.

If you create this culture, you will give yourself the best chance of thriving in today's complicated world.

If You Have a Driver's License, You Know the Basics About Changing and Managing a Culture

Cultures are driven by:

- **A strong common support** *for the end results of your efforts*
- **Shared personal skills** *that everyone understands and uses*
- **Well-understood processes** *that are followed and embraced by all participants*
- **Decision competency** – *people are clear that decisions will be made.*

All four of these elements define the way that cultures work. They can be understood by looking at the way we drive our cars in Seattle's transportation network. If you have a driver's license and drive your car on our different roadways, then you are participating in our region's driving culture – in order to get to your destination, you have to be ALL-IN.

I contend that once you understand that all organizational cultures are built on the four elements, then you can impact any culture by:

- Being consistent in buying ALL-IN to support the desired outcomes of your organization

- Consistently demonstrating the critical individual skills that the ALL-IN Culture defines [e.g.,listening with the intent to understand, not to speak]

- Following the basic ALL-IN processes especially around decision making, conflict management, and initiative processes.

- Making decisions and supporting decisions that are timely and have followed the processes

Let's look at Seattle's driving culture, because the metaphor will help you understand how you can have an impact on any culture.

HOW MANY LANES ARE YOU DRIVING ON?

Cultures are like roadways – you need to know how many lanes you are navigating. Some cultures are two-lane roads: Once you are on the road, you get in behind the person in front of you and make sure you do not rear-end that car.

In most cases, there are places where there are passing lanes and the painted stripes on the road tell you when you can pass or when you can't.

Your individual skill is the personal judgment of how long you have to pass the car in front of you, and how fast you have to go to make the pass. You also have to believe that the cars [obstacles] coming toward you, are using the same rules that you are using.

On the sides of the roads are guardrails that keep you from leaving the roadway, so your only choice is to follow the rules, manage your driving skills and arrive at your destination whenever the road and its traffic allow. This a description of a tightly controlled culture, where staying in the culture requires conformity.

On the other end of the road spectrum: The 4-5 lane freeway, with off-ramps and HOV lanes, heavy traffic congestion, and lots of big trucks. Think of the differences in this type of culture: First, you are no longer concerned with traffic coming at you – the problem is the cars and trucks behind you.

There is also a tendency with this driving experience that you will have more people not making the same individual judgments on how fast they think they can drive – cars changing lanes without using blinkers, and trucks changing lanes just because they can.

In Seattle's driving context, we also have freeway entrances on the wrong side – meaning that in order to get off at the desired exit you have a short distance to

> *Cultures are like roads ways – you need to know how many lanes you are navigating. Some cultures are two-lane roads...*

move across 4-5 lanes in heavy traffic. You may also be on a freeway lane that disappears just at the wrong time.

I have often said that Seattle only has two traffic issues: 1] you can't get ON the freeway and 2] you can't get OFF the freeway – there is nowhere to go. The point is, you may be working in an organizational culture that has many challenges: lots of lanes, lots of traffic, and lots of historical decisions that have engineered work-a-rounds to make things happen.

This is the description of a culture that has not been built with the end in mind. Decisions have been made without clear understanding of how to create

organizational culture -- down the road, traffic will be a mess.

NOW, LET'S LOOK AT ALL-IN FROM THE DRIVER'S POINT OF VIEW:

INDIVIDUAL SKILLS

What does it take to get a driver's license? It starts with the idea that you have to pass a written test on the rules of the road –

In fact, there are studies that suggest we would be safer in self-driving cars than cars driven by human beings.

how to know what the road signs mean, the stripes painted on the roadways, how to pass, how to navigate a yellow light, how to make a turn, using your hazard lights when you stop on the side of the road, parking rules, and on and on.

Then, you usually have a loving relative who takes you to a large parking lot, where you actually drive a car. In my day, we had a stick shift, which meant the highest level of personal skill was starting a car from a dead stop on a steep hill. Today's cars now almost drive themselves.

In fact, there are studies that suggest we would be safer in self-driving cars than cars driven by human beings. [Think of the implications on an organization's culture if computers made

decisions and we just did what we were told.]

Finally, to get your driver's license, you go to the licensing office and you drive the car with a licensor – you have to prove to them that you know the rules of the road and have the skills to drive the car and follow those rules.

Now, think about joining an organization – are you informed on the individual skills that you need to have to be part of the culture? In most cases, there is a handbook and an orientation meeting, at best. How about a mentor to help you understand the culture? What about a job description that defines some interpersonal skills that need to be followed?

Some companies have a 90-day probation period – is it clear what is expected that you demonstrate in those 90 days? My point is that to get a driver's license, there are clear individual expectations – can you define your organization's individual expectations?

FOLLOWING THE PROCESSES

In getting your driver's license you had to know the rules of the road. Does your organization have the processes of their culture clearly articulated?

In most production cultures,

the processes are very defined. Production environments most resemble the two-lane road analogy that I used earlier. They are tightly controlled and have guardrails to ensure that no one leaves the structure of the incremental improvement culture.

Today's world is more about organizational initiatives than incremental change. It's more like my freeway analogy, where the chances for accidents, poor engineering, and miscommunications are very high. Without clear process understanding, you might be in a constant crisis culture. The ALL-IN Culture ensures that the processes in the initiative culture are clear and well understood.

EVERYONE BEING ALL-IN FOR THE ORGANIZATIONAL OUTCOMES

The previous organizational world was built on the concepts of mission, vision, core values, and five-year strategic plans. I contend that the generational differences in our organizational structures have rendered these traditional organizational pillars obsolete; they are no longer a unifying management alternative.

Defining the mission -- is now defining and clarifying outcomes.

Defining the vision -- is now clarifying the initiatives to accomplish the outcomes.

Defining core values -- is now individual skills and organizational processes.

Defining the five-year strategic plan – is now making sure the organizational initiatives are compatible and executed collaboratively.

DECISION COMPETENCY

Decision competency is the outcome, when all of these elements are clear – and followed and respected – and understood as the way that the business is managed. The pace of organizational change is unprecedented; the world is still 20% continuous improvement, but it's now 80% disruptive.

Everything is changing and the previous way of doing things is being disrupted or discontinued by total new ways of doing almost everything. This is the time for a new management vision of how to stay relevant in today's disruptive world.

CLOSING

I love to close any presentation with these thoughts:

- **The largest property rental company** in the world is Airbnb, and they own no properties.
- **The largest travel company** is Expedia, and they own no/ few travel assets.

- **The largest cab company** is Uber, and they own no cabs.

- **The largest retailer** is Amazon, and they own no stores.

- **The largest media company** is Facebook, and they produce no media.

- **The largest video company** is YouTube, and they produce no videos.

- **The largest cable/ satellite companies** will be transformed in the next two years by other online providers.

I could go on, but I contend that every nonprofit/for-profit organization will be confronted with the **change-or-fail dilemma** in the next few years, even in how you drive your car.

Which Would You Rather Have?

A great organizational culture

-OR-

A great organizational strategy

In all the organizations I have been associated with, defining the business strategies has always been a top priority for the management team to focus on.

The development of:

- Vision and mission statements

- Five-year strategic plan

- Branding strategy

- Marketing strategy

- Continuous improvement initiative

- Rewards programs [generally focused on business growth and employee competition]

- Audits, business dashboards, and expense control

These are the primary elements that senior management use to focus the organization on profit and return on investment.

The majority of the meetings and management-to-staff communications revolve around these specific topics.

The major thing that disrupts focus on these elements usually comes in the form of a crisis [something that happens that takes the focus away from these operational strategies].

Human Resource departments play the role of maintaining order, executing the effort

to mitigate employee issues, and maintains the legal responsibilities required by the city, county, state and federal employment laws.

Staying focused on all of these strategies creates the organizational culture. The health of this culture depends on how management interacts with employees while executing all of these operational strategies.

This has been the business operational model for over the last 30 years, and as long as you are in a production business, the model results in growth and achieving profitability goals.

I contend that this business operational model will not continue to work going forward.

The new business focus is being challenged by two specific changes in the demand for products.

FIRST – the fact that we are now in a business climate where product innovation and demand for new forms of products will dominate the focus of every organization, in every product category.

SECOND -- the new majority in the workforce will be Millennials [age 20-35], and the way they work and relate to their business lives will not be compatible with the business strategies of the last 30 years.

What's Next?

In the next 10 years, up to 75% of the current technology will be replaced with a different and more intuitive technology. The Baby Boomers are done consuming and will start to downsize their lifestyles – getting rid of possessions that their children do not want to keep.

The Millennial generation is not consuming the way the Boomers consumed, and, in fact, might be more focused on a minimalist lifestyle.

These factors combine with the fact that for the first time in history, there are now three different generations in the workforce: The Boomers want to stay relevant, but only working part time, the Generation-Xers just want to get things done, and the Millennials have a totally different mindset on how their personal life and their work life should be integrated. They believe that the Boomer lifestyle of "work first, play later," needs to shift so that work and play are equal in importance.

So, what does all this mean in creating a organizational culture going forward? Can you really do a five-year strategic plan? Do

reward programs that reward competition really motivate employees to work harder? Can your workforce adapt to this rapid level of disruptive change? Does cost saving management [continuous improvement] create the innovation that will dominate this new business climate?

Operational strategies during the last 30 years, when our main focus was improving production of consumed products by lowering costs, is now at the end of its business cycle. The next 30 years will be about innovation, and the new consumer products will be created by organizational cultures that are smart and can maximize the impact of continuous change and adaptation – creating new ways

"For the first time in history, there are now three different generations in the workforce."

to accomplish almost everything we do in our society.

In the past 30 years culture was driven by our organizational business strategies.

For the next 30 years culture will drive our organizational business strategies.

For the last 30 years the core

objective of business was creating cheaper products.

For the next 30 years the core objective of business will be innovation of products.

For the last 30 years the Human Resource function was to manage human expenses.

For the next 30 years the Human Resource function will be to hire, retain, and support smart employees that innovate and collaborate to create new value.

The next 30 years will be about an organizational culture that supports

CREATING THE ALL-IN CULTURE

There are four elements to creating an ALL-IN Culture:

1. **All** stakeholders share a relentless ALL-IN to accomplish the organization's mission and desired outcomes.

2. **All** organizational stakeholders are ALL-IN owning and adhering to the organizational process and protocols.

3. **All** organizational stakeholders are ALL-IN understanding the individual leadership and management behaviors that are the foundation for collaborative/innovative cultures.

4. **All** organizational stakeholders are ALL-IN

trusting organizational decision competency.

Innovation is a product of a collaborative organizational culture.

Organizational flexibility only happens when no one ever says: "This is the way we have always done it."

Surviving the next 30 years will require an organizational culture that fosters change and risk, with everyone being ALL-IN to do what's needed.

Going From Being the Cheapest to Being the Smartest

HOW MUCH DOES IT COST TO CHANGE AN ORGANIZATIONAL CULTURE?

CHEAPEST: Relating to low cost or comparatively inexpensive; of, or considered of, small value or poor quality.

SMARTEST: Having or showing intelligence, bright. Canny and shrewd in dealings with others. Energetic or quick in movement.

We are at the end of the business world's love affair with continuous improvement.

We now have made everything into a commodity, and the only real way to evolve in the new world, is to create a culture that can be canny and shrewd in problem solving, and also energetic and quickly adaptable – flexible and open to the changing environment. We have to get smart about it.

Smart can include an element of continuous improvement, but the focus of being smart is to not just provide incremental improvement. This fast-paced new environment will also require being good at fast-paced change.

Being intelligent, as one of my favorite song lyrics states insists that you've got to: "Know when to hold them, know when to fold them – and know when to simply walk away."

Changing cultures may seem like a lot of work and risk -- but I am going to give you three simple activities that I believe will modify/change your culture in six months to a year, with very little cost:

#1: WHAT YOU MEASURE IS WHAT YOU GET

In most organizations, the dashboard of financial ratios gets all of the attention. This

myopic focus on numbers takes a concept like continuous improvement and makes it nothing more than an expense control initiative. So, the first activity is to create an employee survey that will create a culture of smart people who are empowered to suggest new ways to solve a continuous flow of issues and problems.

These 11 questions or indicators define a culture that supports the employees of a smart organization:

1. The things we accomplish positively impact our core mission.

2. Our entire organization frequently celebrates our organizational successes.

3. I am regularly asked to give my opinions and thoughts on important issues confronting our organization.

4. When I offer my opinions, I believe people are trying to understand my point of view.

5. I am comfortable with asking questions and offering my opinion.

6. My supervisor regularly discusses my role/job and I receive understandable feedback on my performance.

7. I work with talented individuals who love to collaborate.

8. We use technology effectively and we receive training and support in using the technology.

9. My organization allows a realistic balance in using my personal social media.

10. My organization has a clear and consistent process for how important decisions are made.

11. Our employee reward program is fair and aligned with my organizational role.

#2: WHAT MANAGEMENT FOCUSES ON, DEFINES THE CULTURE

Think how different your organizational culture would be if it held all management accountable for getting high scores on these 11 questions. I suggest using a 1-5 scale, with 5 being outstanding and 1 being unacceptable. I can tell you that if your scores average 4.5 and above you will have a very smart culture.

If the scores run 4-4.5 you will have an uneven culture with a few people working at it and others not. But the great part of this system is that every manager at every level will have their own dashboard, to define how ALL-IN they are at supporting a smart culture.

If the scores are below a 4.0 average, the organization is going to struggle to adapt to the dynamic waters of our new business environment.

#3: USE OLD SCHOOL SIGNAGE TO DEFINE:

"WE STRIVE TO BE THE SMARTEST IN OUR BUSINESS."

Being THE SMARTEST IN THE BUSINESS is a product of rewarding employees who offer up great new ideas and solutions. They will give you a great score on the employee reward system question and they will serve as the passion and energy source to engage fellow employees in this culture.

WHAT DOES THIS SYSTEM COST?

This is a very simple cultural change concept that WILL COST YOU ALMOST NO CASH.

Cultures are not changed by spending a lot of money – they change because all employees are ALL-IN at behaving with predictable context and focus.

This system focuses on asking the right questions, focusing all management on a dashboard of human value, and visually rewards employees that give their unique ideas and passion to the organization.

How Collaborative is Your Organizational Culture?

WHAT YOU MEASURE AND REWARD IS WHAT YOU GET

The core understanding here is that the continuous improvement initiatives of the past 40 years are different than developing collaborative/innovative organizational cultures.

American business models are shifting from production values toward creation of innovative and game changing products and ideas.

Continuous Improvement cultures are production environments, where organizations are constantly trying to improve performance through incremental process improvement.

Collaborative/innovative cultures are created to find new and radically different ways to solve issues, and these solutions develop a new paradigm. Collaborative/innovative approaches are not incremental – **THEY ARE GAME CHANGERS!**

There are four elements to creating a collaborative/innovative organizational culture:

- **All stakeholders** share a relentless ALL-IN to accomplish the organization's mission and desired outcomes

- **All organizational stakeholders** are ALL-IN owning and adhering to the organizational process and protocols

- **All organizational stakeholders** are ALL-IN understanding the individual leadership and management behaviors that are the foundation for collaborative/innovative cultures

- **All organizational stakeholders** are ALL-IN trusting organizational decision competency

The 10 Cultural Practices that Will Cost You Time, Money, and Talent

1. FOCUSING ON PEOPLE'S ATTITUDES, NOT THEIR BEHAVIORS

In most organizations, there is always someone with what others would define as a "bad attitude." The person or people that have this bad attitude are always viewed as the problem and we spend time trying to find

ways to improve their attitude, which we believe will improve their behaviors. I propose that defining core behaviors and focusing on positively managing those behaviors will create better attitudes. In fact, if behavioral expectations are well-understood and modeled by leadership, the team will self-manage the people with attitude problems, or the people with bad attitudes will leave on their own.

Focus on behavior expectations, not on attitudes.

2. CREATING RULES AND POLICIES TO MANAGE THE EXCEPTION

Anytime you have a group of people working together, someone will do something that seems very stupid and way out of line. When this occurs, managers are confronted with a basic dilemma of how to deal with the problem. Of course, this becomes the most visible demonstration of a manager's skill at dealing with an employee performance issue.

Once the issue is resolved, the next question is how to ensure that this will never happen again. Creating a new rule or policy that you believe will ensure that this exception will never happen again sends a message to all the other team members that they are not trusted to be smart enough to know this was stupid. Now mutual trust takes a hit.

Over time, if every employee bad action turns into a new rule and/or policy, the culture will spend all the time on preventing stupid behaviors vs. valuing good behaviors. Trust will fade away and compliance will deteriorate passion.

Deal with the exception, but don't make everyone pay the price for one stupid exception.

3. NOT DEALING WITH CONFLICT

Conflict is a basic human activity, an activity that very few people like to participate in. But conflict is a core activity that allows progress to be made.

If an organization has no conflict – I contend that it will eventually fail.

Conflict often creates tension and passion about direction and activities. It can provide the energy for productive change and collaboration.

Remember three thoughts about managing conflict:

1. Make sure you are having a discussion about the same problem.

2. Let all of the passion be expressed before you start

looking for solutions.

3. Find a short-term solution [the more the passion, the shorter the time frame].

Organizations that deal with conflicts regularly grow and change; organizations that don't deal with conflicts stagnate and perish.

4. REWARD PROGRAMS THAT REWARD THE WRONG THINGS

Baby Boomers love competition, so most organizations being managed by Boomers have competitions. This kind of incentivizing may have worked in the past, but with three different generations in the current workforce, it no longer motivates people to compete.

The idea that competitive earned rewards will motivate people's energy no longer works.

One of my favorite questions to ask is: Are your performance measurements and performance rewards actually reflecting your effectiveness? In most of the responses, I get the answer no.

There are several things that have made rewards programs obsolete:

• The reward program was designed to increase some activity that drives top-line sales or bottom-line profits. Not everyone has the actual control of the factors that

accomplish either of these two outcomes.

• The reward program has little relationship to an employee's job description or annual review.

• When you talk about competition, there may be a winner, but everyone else is a loser.

The new world is giving rewards to people that behave and perform to the role they play in their collaborative environment, not because they beat their fellow employees.

5. THE FOCUS IS ON FIXING PROBLEMS, NOT DRIVING STRENGTHS

Organizations/people have a pre-disposed focus on fixing an organizational problem. Everyone likes to talk about what we could do better. In many cases, they want to talk about what YOU could do better.

Growth is focused on what we could be doing rather than on what we are doing. Organizational focus starts with maximizing what we are good at, and making sure that we maximize our strengths – not on achieving something new. Maximizing strengths is about What that is and How we do it. Fixing something or chasing something new is about Why we need to do it, and the vision of what success looks like.

Drive your strengths, before you change directions.

6. NOT FOCUSING ON HUMAN COMMUNICATIONS SKILLS

To be a great organization, you have to establish a culture that never says these words;

"I THOUGHT WE TALKED ABOUT THIS"

The best way to understand if your culture is working well is when all individuals take accountability for great interpersonal communications skills.

There are three basic elements of this interpersonal communications effort:

- All individuals listen with the intent to understand, not just waiting for a space to speak.

- It is the sender's responsibility to send a clear message. It is the receiver's responsibility to institute mutual understanding. When in doubt, it is the sender's responsibility to make sure the message was understood.

- Everyone has the responsibility to make sure everyone understands what success looks like.

> *Great organizations know that without great individual communication behaviors, you can't be a great organization!*

7. NOT UNDERSTANDING GENERATIONAL DIFFERENCES IN ATTITUDES AND MOTIVATIONS

For the first time in human history, there are three generations working together: The Baby Boomers, The Generation-Xers, and NOW here come the Millennials. Each of the three generations has different views about the world and how one should be involved in the workforce.

Baby Boomers are optimistic and competitive, Gen-Xers are skeptical and very independent, and Millennials have strong technical skills and a whole new way to be social. The only way to get all three generations engaged and on the same page is to build a collaborative organizational culture. The world is now about attracting and keeping human talent.

Without Millennials in your organization, you can't understand the largest audience in the country.

8. NOT MAKING QUALITY DECISIONS

Organizations have to make decisions, and in today's world of mega-data, the preferred conversation revolves around, "What does the data tell us?" Data is a start, but the reality is that decisions impact the people in the organization and without other parameters, you may make a data-driven decision that nobody understands or is passionate about.

When making a decision, first decide upon the last day that the decision can be made. Remember all great decisions are made on the last day; why would you make an important decision before you have to? Make sure that you have factored the human component into any decision that will impact the organization's people.

Finally, make sure you spend time explaining: What the decision was, Why the decision was made that way, When the decision goes into effect, Who is most impacted, and How the decision will be implemented.

Decisions have a huge impact on an organization's culture. Make sure they present a clear vision of what success looks like going forward.

> *"Many times, the initial problem was caused by a solution to an earlier problem..."*

9. HAVING AN ANSWER WITHOUT A CLEAR UNDERSTANDING OF THE PROBLEM

With interactions in collaborative cultures, the effort is to let individuals "weigh in" and give opinions and thoughts about solutions before a decision is made. Allowing input without facilitation skills can create expectations that can't be fulfilled; make sure that the problem being discussed is very clear.

I love to sit in brainstorming meetings and listen to people throw out solutions to what they perceive as the problem – in most cases, individuals are giving solutions to a bunch of different problems.

Always be sure to write out the problem and ensure that everyone is clear as to what the problem is. Many times, the initial problem was caused by a solution to an earlier problem, so always ask the second question: Why is this a problem?.

Never decide a solution before you clearly define the problem, and always ask, "Why is this a problem?"

10. NOT HIRING THE RIGHT PEOPLE

Hiring the right people will always be better than dealing with poor performing employees later. Hiring the right people, will always help create a better culture than hiring someone that does not fit in.

There are lots of thoughts about how to do this, but here are a few suggestions that I believe might help: A) Hire for the talents and personality of the individual, not the work experience. Just because they have done it before does not mean they will fit in your culture. B) Find out if they are very curious. Curious people will fuel passion and not be afraid of change. C) Figure out if they are empathic. To be collaborative, people need to be able to understand the needs and issues of others. D) Look to see if they are fun to play with. Collaboration needs to be fun.

Personality – Talents – Curiosity – Empathic Skills – and Fun

People with these traits will figure out how to play in collaborative sandbox – and innovation and adaptation will be the outcome.

The Eight Interpersonal Behavioral Skills That Build Trust

DID YOU KNOW THAT YOU ACTUALLY TRUST EVERYONE YOU WORK WITH?!

You trust them to be late – to be funny – to be slow – to be inaccurate – to be the person that you have come to expect them to be. You see, trust is about associates acting in accordance with your expectations of their usual behavior.

It actually can get worse: Research suggests that within 20 seconds of meeting someone, you form your opinion of that person, and then only see those behaviors that reinforce your initial opinion. In Steven Covey's book, *The Speed of Trust,* he suggests that high levels of trust create the ability to move faster in making agreements and getting things done.

He is right – not only on getting things done, but also on getting nothing done. So, positive trust is very important. The following eight behaviors are my core practices that accelerate the building of positive levels of trust. But in collaborative cultures, trust only acts as the doorway to respect. High levels of positive trust get you to

respect, and respect gets you to collaboration and innovation.

If you want to be innovative as a culture, you need both TRUST and RESPECT.

IT ALL STARTS WITH A CONVERSATION

CONVERSATION: A form of interactive spontaneous communication between two or more people who are following the rules of etiquette. It's a polite give and take of subject thought by talking with each other for company.

How well do you engage individuals and small groups in conversation that allows for equal exchange of information?

How comfortable are you engaging considering the time pressures of your workday?

Score your behavior 1-10, with 10 being very good.

ASKING THE RIGHT QUESTIONS

QUESTIONS: Linguistic expression to make a request for information. The skill of asking right questions; categorically looking for straightforward answers or basic information; analytical-qualified answers [defining or re-defining information].

Do you ask questions and show an inquisitive nature with clients?

How well do you use a question that engages individuals and or groups at the level of relationship that best enhances the depth of those relationships?

Score your behavior 1-10 with 10 being very good.

DEMONSTRATING THE LISTENING TOUCH

ACTIVE LISTENING: Requires the listener to repeat what they have heard to the speaker by way of re-stating or paraphrasing what they have heard in their own words.

How Often do you Actively Listen vs. Waiting to Speak?

Do you set aside time to listen during conversations?

Score your behavior 1-10 with 10 being very good.

DEMONSTRATING EMPATHY AND RESPECT

EMPATHY: The capacity to recognize emotions that are being experienced by another person. The ability to imagine one's self as the other person.

RESPECT: A positive feeling of esteem or deference for a person or group. It is something that is earned by the standards of the society in which one lives.

Respect cannot be bought or traded – it is built and earned over time.

How consistently do you show respect and empathy to individuals and groups that you work with?

Score your behavior 1-10 with 10 being very good.

BEING VERY GOOD AT EXPLAINING AND EDUCATING

EXPLANATION: A set of statements constructed to describe a set of facts, which clarify the causes, content, and consequences of those facts. Explanation is subject to interpretation and discussion.

EDUCATION: In its general sense, a form of learning in which knowledge, skills, and habits of a group of people are transferred to another individual or group.

How good you are at explaining and educating?

Score your behavior 1-10 with 10 being very good.

MANAGING EXPECTATIONS AND CREATING CLEAR AGREEMENTS

EXPECTATIONS: In uncertainty, expectation is what is considered the most likely to happen. It is a belief that is centered on the future. If something happens that is not expected, it is a surprise. An expectation is about the behavior or performance of another person.

GENTLEMAN'S AGREEMENT: An informal agreement between two or more parties. It is typically oral, though it may be written. The essence of a gentleman's agreement is that it relies upon the honor of the parties for its fulfillment.

How consistently do you define, clarify, and/or establish clear expectations and mutual understanding with your business relationships?

Score your behavior 1-10 with 10 being very good.

DEALING WITH CONFLICT

CONFLICT: The mental struggle resulting from incompatible or opposing need, drive, wishes – external or internal demands. It is this opposition between people that gives rise to drama or friction.

How well do you deal with conflict? Do you have a specific strategy to handle conflict?

Score your behavior 1-10 with 10 being very good.

ASKING FOR AND TAKING FEEDBACK

FEEDBACK: The return to the point of evaluation or corrective behavior about an action or process. Helping to get valuable information about the impact of these behavioral skills on your business partners' level of trust in the relationship.

Do you regularly ask for and or receive feedback from your business partners and clients?

Does asking for feedback seem like a practical or contrary idea?

Score your behavior 1-10 with 10 being very good.

CONCLUSION

ADD UP YOUR SCORES: 90%=72, 80%=64, 70%=56, and 60%=48

None of these interpersonal skills are hard to do, they just require being conscious of doing them and becoming aware that if you do:

Trust in your business relationships will set you apart from all your competition, increase your bottom line, and gain you the hardest thing to achieve in life: Respect.

Culture Change can Happen at any Level of an Organization

Last week I had the opportunity to speak to a group of 100 individuals who manage the ticket sales for major university athletic departments across the country. It was one of the first times I was giving a speech, not facilitating a small group discussion. I was given a one-hour time slot, but was positioned at 11 a.m. – I was the only thing between them and lunch. My topic, of course, was How to Build an ALL-IN Culture.

I started the conversation by asking three questions:

1. How important is an organization's culture to the group's output?

2. How important is an organizational culture to their personal well-being?

3. Were they working in a culture they liked?

For the first two questions everyone raised their hands, but on the third question only a small number of hands were raised.

The ticket business is a very difficult business – in most cases, demand for tickets is determined by the whether the university's

athletic teams are winning or not. There has also been a large increase in exposure on TV, which has changed the traditional game day experience dramatically.

Games are now more associated with a television schedule than with fans in the stadium. The ticket operations staff are feeling a lot of pressure – to not only be very good at processing the tickets they sell, but also they now have the added responsibly of re-selling or recapturing past ticket buyers who have decided to watch the games on TV.

As I started working my way through the concepts of how you build trust and respect, building the baseline of outstanding cultures, I was struck that I have always viewed this as a process that needed to be supported by the senior management of an organization.

Changing an organization's culture requires that the senior group drives this process, yet here I was talking to the managers in the middle of the organization – who are not going to see or feel this type of change driven by their athletic department's leadership.

About two-thirds of the way through detailing the 8-10 behaviors that build positive trust and respect, I found myself wondering if my impassioned pitch was just a pipe dream or if a manager or even a non-manager could use these behavior concepts to create their own personal cultures – and if they demonstrated these behaviors, how this might create a cultural change that did not need to be driven from the top of the organization.

As I reached the close of the presentation, I had this very clear understanding: An individual can create his or her own culture by simply following the basics of the behavioral skills approach.

If you listen with the intent to understand and use paraphrasing and great questions as your way of actually listening to another team member, you will develop the reputation of being a great listener. People will want to talk to you.

If you are the person in the meeting who clarifies the problem before everyone argues about the solutions, people will want you to be in meetings because you are impacting the outcome and helping to focus the meeting.

If you always do an initiative document that addresses the five W's [What?, Why?, When?, Where?, Who?], and a short How – and you always have the Whos sign off on the initiative – you will be the one who gets projects done, with less argument and more ownership.

If you manage conflicts in a skillful manner, you will be the one who other people want in the room when conflict arises.

If you are the person who works very hard at expressing clear expectations, both for yourself as well as for others, you will be the person that others will want to partner with on projects.

If you regularly [at least once per year] pull out your job description and make sure your tasks on the description actually match what you do – and you

"By following the behavioral principles in the All-IN Culture, you can gain control of your position..."

make sure that your boss agrees with your changes – you will be the one in control of your position, and your boss will be aware of your discipline and attention to doing a good job.

By following the behavioral principles in the ALL-IN Culture, you can gain control of your position, and you will find that other people who you work with will start following your leadership.

Culture change happens when people's behaviors change – attitude follows the behaviors, and people want to trust and respect individuals who are skilled at behaving in an ALL-IN manner.

Understanding the Problem Before Deciding on a Solution

Solving problems is at the core of all organizational behavior. Many timees I've heard, "If not for the problems, I wouldn't be needed." Management is all about problem solving; so where do we start? Problem solving requires several basic processes:

- A group needs to have some practical wisdom, looking at issues with enough experience and applied understanding of the factors that will be impacted, as solutions become understood.

- A group needs to have a passion for clarity, making sure that solutions are actually viable to solve the problem at hand.

Being relentless at defining the problem and understanding Why it has become the problem is 50% of finding solutions. Two stories come to mind as examples of this process.

Changing the Bon Marché Service Culture:

The Bon was trying to reposition itself – having been founded on value in the late 1800s, the company had a long history and owned this segment of the retail market.

Throughout the late 1960s, this was a good position to be in, but the world was changing and this position was losing ground to the growing middle class, and to consumers who were no longer only focused on value. They were now looking for style and fashion.

The problem was clear: We had to change to a different market position.

This transformation required a total rethinking about merchandise, visual display, classification adjacencies, marketing, and customer service. We needed to find new solutions to make this market position change.

I was in charge of the customer service element, and also the marketing component. This is where I first learned about the concept that behaviors were more important than attitudes.

We were doing mystery shopper reports in each of the 40+ stores, but the reports were not changing behaviors of the customer service associates. The associates viewed the reports as management punishment, not as a helping tool to understand our level of service.

We needed to have a service culture, and people's attitudes became the issue. It was the Why we were doing these reports that was not understood.

> *The solution was coming from the top layer of management, but it was not owned by the people doing the service.*

I asked for 5,000 labor hours, and had each employee of the company do our mystery shopper report on a competitor of their choice. It only took a couple of weeks for the entire organization to not only understand the service concept, but also to become proud of our new service standard.

The problem was a defined corporate problem, but the solution was to transfer the ownership of service to the people. We knew the problem, but we missed Why the problem existed. The problem existed because the people did not own the answer, and until we empowered them to own the answer we could not make our solution work.

The Sheriff's 911 Call Center:

I was asked to help figure out why the King County Sheriff's

911 Call Center had such high turnover. Call center employee turnover is very expensive – it takes over a year to hire, train, mentor, and certify that a new call receiver can work without supervision. You can imagine how all this time adds up. The effort was driven by defining the problem and understanding why it was the problem.

After interviewing the entire workforce through individual conversation and group meetings, the conversations always went to certain individuals who bullied other employees.

One call receiver told the story that if she had to transfer information to the dispatcher working the south part of King County, that the package of information had to be different from how the information was packaged to the north dispatcher.

I regularly heard the words, "I wasn't trained that way." The problem became very clear – the way people were trained was different, depending upon When you were trained and Who trained you. Managers, trainers

and mentors all had different approaches to answering calls, the packaging of information, and intensity of the problem.

All of this was in a performance environment where, with a high priority call, the call receiver had 10 seconds to answer the call, and then 40 seconds to determine the level of danger and package the information to the dispatcher, so the dispatcher could send the appropriate law enforcement officers – lots of urgency and high levels of stress.

This dynamic created a level of turnover that was making things worse. The problem was clear – we needed to establish a more standardized approach to each of the five communication interactions involved – with the most important being: The caller to the call receiver, and the call receiver to the dispatcher.

Why was this happening?

The answer was in the way that call receivers were being judged for their performance – how they were graded and reviewed. The call center used a quality assurance audit, where the shift managers would listen to a recorded interaction of a call receiver and a caller, and give the grades based upon 15 Yes/No questions. One of the questions was: Answered the call correctly?, while another was: Managed the call correctly?

The first question involved

saying the scripted opening line when a call came in; the second question was more about the Art of 911 Call Receiving. This QA audit was Why there was high turnover – Yes/No is easy for the first question. But the issue of the art and technique of handling the call is not black and white. How you handle a car accident is one thing – how you handle a domestic violence call is much different.

I rewrote the quality assurance audit and created two different scales of answers. There were six Yes/No questions, and eight 1-5 questions [1 being very poor and 5 being very good]. I then had the 26 people that either trained, mentored, or managed the call receivers listen to the same two phone calls.

The first was a car accident and the second was a domestic violence call. I am sure you can guess what happened: Almost everyone judged the Yes/ No questions the same, but here was total disagreement when it came to the scoring of the 1-5 questions. The lack of consistency in how people were trained and reviewed caused high turnover, and until they all could see it was "their problem," they could just blame the people with the bad attitudes.

> *Organizational culture is based upon ownership of individual behaviors and processes that everyone supports.*

Using the line, "This is the way we do things around here" had better be clear to all stakeholders, not just a few. Always define the problem, and always understand Why the problem exists before you try a solution.

The Art of Making Decisions

One of the first things you learn as a new manager is that you have to make decisions – decisions about a whole range of issues and employee activities. You are constantly asked for special exemptions for the work schedule – or priorities as to what is more important to accomplish first. So, what is the definition of a decision and how do you gain the confidence to make decisions at the right pace, based on the right amount of process?

Decision-making can be regarded as the cognitive process resulting in the selection of a belief or a course of action from among several possibilities.

Every decision-making process produces a final choice. Participation allows individuals and groups to influence the decision in a representative manner.

In some ways you actually have three possible behaviors for making a decision:

1. You can choose to make a decision.

2. You can choose to not make a decision.

3. And finally, you can choose to do nothing and see what happens.

In the mid-1970s, I was promoted to the position of divisional merchandise manager for the Bon Marché – a 45-unit department store.

At the age of 28 I replaced a long-term merchant who was responsible for what had been the backbone of department store merchandise: Records, Books, Toys, Luggage, Sporting Goods, Stationary, Housewares, Lamps, Pictures, Mirrors, and Drugs.

I was assigned 10 buyers and their departmental staff, for a total of 25 employees.

So there I was – the MBA young gun taking over for a long-time employee, with the merchandise that was just starting to transition to new avenues of retail, beginning the boom of building Classification Superstores.

On top of that, the company had decided to move all of these merchandise classifications from the main floor to the 8th floor. I was told to figure out a way to maintain the business volume and to make a small profit: Challenge On!

"Though the challenge was exciting, I quickly discovered that the hardest part of this process was learning how to make decisions."

All of my buyers were 15-25 years older than me – had families – and were very nervous on how this "kid" was going to operate these very traditional department store businesses.

It did not take long for me to feel very uncomfortable knowing that my decisions could have a profound impact on all of these people's lives – knowing that my staff had been doing these jobs and developing market relationships for many years – and I had only three years of experience being a buyer.

I spent some sleepless nights thinking about how I should handle this dilemma. My personality is positive and confident, but I must admit this situation tested my value system and my will to succeed. This high-pressure environment created some tense moments.

As I tackled this dilemma, I found a process that I could use as a consistent and well-understood culture behavior. It became the central tool I used – not only in maintaining a productive culture, but in managing a group of people into a collaborative working environment that grew the businesses and was also a way to make money.

As more and more decisions were being put on my plate, I came to understand the fine balance between getting input and buy-in, incorporating the fact that I had to make decisions – it was my job.

The process became the cultural element that all of the staff members could trust I would follow, and they all knew in the end that if they followed the process, most of the time it would lead to a decision that they could actively support. The process was really quite simple; every time I had a decision to make, I would follow this set of behaviors:

1. I would try to clarify the problem we were discussing and making decisions about.

2. Once defined, I would get three opinions. When possible I would let the senior buyers help me to "source" where the opinions came from. *This helped engage them in the process*

3. The most important aspect of this process/conclusion:

   • If all three opinions were the same, there was an obvious answer to the problem.

- If all three opinions were different, then there was still some discovery required.

- If there were two opinions the same and one different, then I placed a value on the third opinion, to decide if one more opinion was needed.

4. I then made the decision, now able to define Why I had made the decision, and the senior buyers all trusted that the process had been followed. The consistency of this process allowed the whole team to understand how decisions were made – and I could be confident knowing that the team was supportive, and would follow through on executing the decision.

5. There was an unintended consequence to this process: If the decision did not prove to be right, there was no second guessing or blaming. The process had been followed and we just moved on to make the next decision.

My goal is to give the reader tangible behaviors and activities that will help build a work culture with high production and cooperation, which then creates long-term loyalty and evangelism for the environment. Here is a list of my core thoughts about THE ART OF MAKING DECISIONS:

> *Start by making sure you have clearly defined the problem or issue. Never assume that everyone knows what the problem/issue really is.*

- If you can't describe/write the problem in a single sentence and have people read it with mutual understanding, the process will fail.

- Clearly define the process that you will always [unless you can't] try to follow.

- My process was getting three opinions – and getting staff to drive where the opinions came from. This gave them ownership, not only within the process, but also helped to drive support for the outcome.

- Always define the results of the process, and inform staff of the decision. For important decisions in particular, make sure that everyone is informed on What the decision was and Why you made this decision.

Meetings and the One-pager

Once a decision is made, use the opportunity to convert the *process* into an action plan. Allow and encourage people to speak and ask questions about what

happens next.

Create a short written document that defines the answer to the five W's and one H [What?, Why?, When?, Where?, Who?, and a short How?]. Always use the word DRAFT for discussion, this allows people to see that this is not just a decision – it is the start of putting the decision into action.

Impacted individuals should always have a personal conversation. In many decisions of importance, specific individuals are impacted more than others. Meet with these people before the decision is announced.

Explain the What and Why – describe the process and let them have the final word. You will know this process works when they become active supporters, not passively resistant.

THE ART OF MAKING DECISIONS

There is an art to this. Done well and with confidence, this process should transfer ownership, create passion, and drive execution toward the solution to the problem that you clearly defined during the first step in the process.

Final Thoughts

As a manager, it is your job to manage decisions – small and large – and the behaviors you choose to use in this process will have a disproportionate influence on the nature of your group's culture.

So remember two outliers to this discussion:

1. No matter what you intended to happen with your decisions, the unintended consequences will win the day.

2. No matter how hard you try – *ALL GREAT DECISIONS WILL TEND TO BE MADE ON THE LAST DAY!!* But remember, hard decisions need time.

Always know when the last day is!

All Great Decisions are Made on the Last Day

No matter how many times I needed an important decision made, either in business or in my personal life, it seemed I could never get someone to react until the last moment.

There were always reasons and problems in getting someone else to make a decision in what I felt was an appropriate time frame.

As I rose higher in a bureaucracy I, myself, was confronted with people who suggested that I make more timely decisions. They wanted to know why I couldn't be more decisive, and I realized that whether in business or personal life, it always ended up that all great decisions were made on the last day. There was really no reason to make a decision until some time pressure had been placed upon the situation.

Even more interesting than when decisions were made was what process I was using to make them. Was it just that it was the last day, and time to make up my mind? What if I was wrong? Would someone ask me later

why I had made a decision and I would simply answer that it was the last day? With all of these thoughts, I had to come up with a process that would give me the best chance of making a good decision and allow me to proceed with confidence – because the worst mistake a manager can make is to second guess his or her own decision.

I discovered a few simple rules I could follow to enhance my self-confidence. I thought that if I trained my people to follow them, they too would become more self-confident. In the case of a decision that didn't work, we would not place blame, but move on to make a new decision.

> *"...whether in business or personal life, it always ended up that all great decisions were made on the last day."*

THE RULES

The first rule is to determine the last date a decision can be made. It is very important to establish dates and understand why they were picked. In many cases decisions have one date by which a go-no/go mentality costs no money, with costs escalating after that date. Managers who know their technical business understand this late decision, cost-of-business relationship.

The second rule is that there are no bad decisions, only decisions

that don't work out. If a decision does not work out, the only problem is that a new direction has not been taken.

In other words, never look back once you choose a course of action.

And proceed with confidence, but don't become so focused that when it is obviously not working you continue in stupidity. One must always remember that, "If we continue in our current direction we will most likely end up where we are headed." If you don't like where you are headed, change direction.

The third rule is always get three opinions, bids, or discussions on any important decision. I was constantly confronted with questioning whether my decisions were appropriate and correct. I found out that if I get three opinions on any subject, one of three things happens.

THE HAPPENINGS

The first is that all three opinions are the same. This always makes me feel that if there is a better idea or price, it is not readily evident; therefore, continued search would delay a decision that has no option.

The second possibility is that all three opinions are different. In this case, it is open season. I should continue to search until I have a better understanding or opinion as to what the best solution might be.

The last possibility is that two of the three say the same thing, but the third person has a different idea. There are many options to this discussion: You can choose to get more opinions, or, because of time constraints, go with your gut feeling – knowing you may not know all of the options. The fact that you thought about this decision and got three opinions enhances your confidence because at least the decision went through some process.

The real value in this process is that whenever I follow my own advice and get my three opinions, I proceed with decisions in a confident and comfortable manner. If a decision does not work out, I still know that it was a good one. I then use the process to make a new decision.

A manager's job is to make decisions.

If you use this process, there are no bad decisions, only decisions that don't work out. And the only real problem is if you choose not to make a new decision.

How Will Your Organization Handle Disruption??

DISRUPTION: A disturbance or problem that interrupts an event, activity, or process.

In previous sections, I have tried to build a case for the idea that our current and future world will be full of rapid change that will disrupt the current way that organizations operate.
We have arrived at the place

> *"It is projected that 75-80 % of how we use technology today will be obsolete in the next 10 years – and maybe faster."*

where businesses are no longer looking for incremental change; we now want a new product that disrupts the existing way we are doing things. The new success is to make something obsolete.

Thomas Friedman [a regular columnist for *The New York Times*] authored an editorial worth some further thought. The title of the editorial was, *"Hillary, Jeb, Facebook and Disorder."*

Friedman's main point was that we have a lot of important issues to grapple with, and that in our current political environment, no politicians are talking about the "Elephant in the Room" – our world being disrupted.

SOME OF HIS KEY OBSERVATIONS:

We are redefining the social contracts between governments and their citizens as well as employers and their employees. Issues like the trade deals, immigration, having three generations in the workforce at one time, Baby Boomers retiring, and the state of our health care system, just to name a few.

The massive change in our use of technology. We are now in a period where there are no limitations to computing power. We have no digital storage issues, we have no bandwidth constraints, and networking, sensor, and software generation are exploding.

It is projected that 75-80% of how we use technology today will be obsolete in the next 10 years – and maybe faster.

> *Some of our planet's most brilliant individuals think that our biggest issue is that now computers are smarter than humans.*

Jobs are endangered. In the trade deals of the past the driver seemed to be finding cheap

happening."

There sure is. We're at the start of a major shift on the question

> ***"...47% of US jobs are at high risk of becoming taken over by smart machines and software in the next 20 years."***

production, which changed the country's job opportunities.

Now, with the massive increase in computing power, Friedman quotes a recent Oxford Martin School study that concluded that, "47% of U.S. jobs are at high risk of becoming taken over by smart machines and software in the next 20 years."

> *Knowledge workers at the middle or top may be more threatened than those doing physical work."*

What is worth owning? Friedman quotes from an essay by Tom Goodman, an executive of Havas Media:

"Uber, the world's largest taxi company, owns no vehicles. Facebook, the world's most popular media owner, creates no content. Alibaba, the most valuable retailer, has no inventory. And Airbnb, the world's largest accommodation provider, owns no real estate. Something interesting is

of what's worth owning.

What each of the above companies have in common is that they have either created trust platforms that match supply and demand for things people never thought of supplying: A spare bedroom in their home or a seat in their car or a commercial link between a small retailer in North Dakota and a small manufacturer in China.

Or they are behavioral platforms that spin off extremely valuable data for retailers and advertisers. Or they are behavioral platforms on which ordinary people can generate reputations – for driving, hosting or any skill you can imagine – and then market themselves globally.

WE ARE LEAVING THE WORLD OF MACRO CONTROL AND MOVING TO THE WORLD OF MICRO...

What will a world of migrating people look like?

People all over the globe are starting to migrate from one place to another. At this point the migration is being fueled by people leaving "Disorder

Zones" and hoping to find "Order Zones." All over the Middle East and North Africa, Africans and Arabs are trying to get to Europe.

People in Myanmar and Bangladesh are trying to get to Thailand and Malaysia. Central American parents are sending their kids to the United States. Last year, the UN's refugee agency said that more than 50 million people were displaced – more than any time since World War II.

> *What happens over the next few years if the drought in California continues, and Boston continues to have winters with 108 inches of snow?*

Migration is no longer East to West or Capitalism vs. Communism.

What will be the impact of a warmer planet?

> *"…I will just keep my head down and react when I need to react."*

Migration is one of the possibilities – but what about our food chain, or the fact that Florida might lose the Everglades due to higher ocean water levels?

At this point, I am sure you are thinking, "These things are so out of my control, I will just keep my head down and react when I need to react."

That is one way to respond to the complexity of these issues. Another option is to work toward creating an organizational culture that collaborates, and can adapt and make small adjustments, in order to be better able to respond to more destructive disruptions.

Here is one example:

Let's look at the probability of your organization needing to implement a new level of technology – one that you have never seen before. Let's assume that you have tried to implement a mobile business application, but never really made this initiative an imperative. Your business culture did not fully adapt to mobile technology and embrace the change in methodology and technology.

Now it is a new disruptive factor in your business strategy, you will either have to adapt with a big leap in technology, or lose your business to competition that is using this application to its fullest.

Building an organizational culture that can adapt to change will help manage the distinct possibility of a major disruption to your business model that you are not prepared for.

When you look back to the chance you had to create a culture that was able to migrate to the previous mobile app, you might be better positioned to make the kind of incremental organizational changes, to handle this new disruption.

Friedman concludes his editorial by paraphrasing Trotsky once more:

"You may not be interested in talking about the future, but the future will be interested in talking to you!"

Managing Conflict

No matter how long you have been managing, there is a tendency to be uneasy with the amount of conflict inherent in a political, bureaucratic environment.

In some bureaucracies, the nature of conflict becomes quite personal and is taken to a level that can destroy any chance of teamwork or community spirit.

When you are confronted with this type of environment, you had better have a strong sense of yourself and a great sense of your skills and strengths.

It is highly likely that the people you are dealing with in this environment are very insecure. They are only comfortable when putting others down, and place other people below themselves to ensure that they feel in

"...most big companies, and many small ones, are made up of competitive people..."

control. In this type of culture it is very hard to determine the group's common mission or focus.

Usually the entire organization's success is dependent upon an environment in which one-upmanship and competitive conflict are the motivating factors.

I am not suggesting that all organizations have cultures like this, but I do believe that most big companies, and many small ones, are made up of competitive people. I remain amazed at the overall tendency of American culture to promote insecurity in employees.

The basic **"perform or get fired"** mentality tends to create an insecure senior management – and as we all know, most things travel downhill from there. The point of this discussion is not to suggest that all American employees suffer from massive

insecurity, but to clarify that if there are even a few such people in your working environment, it is probable that you will have some personnel conflicts. No matter what the degree, the word "conflict" implies differences of opinion, and is a fundamental part of the management process.

There are some basic steps that, if followed, allow you the best opportunity to not only survive in an atmosphere of conflict, but to break through and be consistently effective at negotiating and acquiring agreements. These steps work for any negotiating you may do, and with practice, become a basic style that will work in all parts of your life.

THE BASIC STEPS

Step 1:

Clarify what the discussion is about.

In any emotional discussion, people become polarized beyond the real level of their thoughts. How many times have you been in a conversation when somebody pushed your button and the next thing you know you're at complete odds with them, defending a position that is not really representative of what you believe?

Your ability to stay focused on defining the key issue can save you a tremendous amount of time and emotion, and is essential in making sure the

conflict is resolved.

Step 2:

Get the other person's position out first.

There is a principle that states, "There is a small difference between being very skilled and being manipulative." I believe that being skilled means that in many ways you are going to manipulate the situation to your

> ***"...conflict resolution is dependent upon getting the emotions out first."***

advantage.

Getting the other person's feelings and opinions on the table first leaves you in a very important position – you will still own your position and emotions. This allows you to be in control of the conflict and manage the resolution of the issue.

There is a second, and more important, concept that you must be able to handle: Conflict resolution is dependent upon getting the emotions out first. Emotional people do not agree to do anything except remain emotional. It's okay to leave the process stuck in emotion for as long as necessary to get the emotion out and over with. In most instances people will move through emotion by talking about it, telling somebody about

it, or writing it down. The fact that emotional people don't make good decisions or good partners is true; make sure the emotion is on the table or you are wasting your time going on.

Step 3:

Explain your position and remove your emotion.

Much of the above conversation also must be applied to yourself. If you are carrying a great deal of emotion and you want a solution to really work, it is important to make sure you have no hidden agendas. Much of this discussion is dependent upon your skill level and your beliefs, trust, and respect toward the person you are dealing with.

Step 4:

Agree on something.

The turning point in any conflict is that moment when the issue

> *"The thing that you agree upon is not as important as the fact that you've agreed to something."*

is clear and the emotion is out. At this point, people are usually ready to go forward. The important part is to find some idea you can agree on. It can be as simple as agreeing that you have to find some way to work together.

The thing that you agree upon is not as important as the fact that you've agreed to something. There is an old sales approach that says in order to get somebody to say yes, you start with a small agreement and continue to build a series of them until you ask for agreement on the big question. This technique is similar to that. Start by agreeing on something to build a base for a more lasting agreement.

Step 5:

Brainstorm possible solutions.

At this point it's time to start thinking of how the issue can be resolved. It is important that both sides feel their offered solutions have been heard. Even if you already have a solution to the conflict, it is very important to allow the other party to participate in deciding what the answer will be.

Step 6:

Try the agreed-upon solution for a limited time period.

Once you have discussed possible solutions, pick one. The solution itself is not as important to the overall outcome as the process. Don't try to force it as "The Solution." The important part is to agree to try the solution for a short period of time.

You have to give trust to get trust, and it is very hard to trust a long-term solution without some time for adjustment. People can agree and commit to short-term solutions with much greater comfort and energy than to long-term agreements.

Step 7:

What does success look like?

In reading this collection of writings, you already know my emphasis on defining a clear picture of success. Understanding how you will know you have arrived at the end of the journey is the only way you can get there.

Choosing a solution and deciding to try it for a period of time helps, but having a clear picture of what it feels and acts like when it is working is paramount in building trust and confidence – in both the conflict resolution model and in a trusting and respectful relationship.

Conflict is inherent in all organizations and relationships.

Feeling that you can control the conflicts in your life without them controlling you is a basic building block of self-esteem. The ability to understand the process of conflict resolution allows you to be a strong player in any environment.

The Three Types of Functional Management

Every day, bureaucrats are challenged with changing priorities brought about by the dynamics of the overall business environment. During periods of accelerated change, these priorities seem to be more difficult to define, and change from one moment to the next. Bureaucrats also tend to want a high degree of control over their time and the time of the people who work for them. This entire dynamic of changes can cause larger and larger amounts of stress, and in the end, have profound effects on the overall morale of any work group.

The fundamental tools for handling these changes are a management framework and a basic understanding of the three types of functional management. The ultimate goal is to be able to control the change process by knowing when and how they should be used.

CRISIS MANAGEMENT

The first type of management is crisis management. This happens when there is a strong possibility that a significant task will not get completed and the manager decides to increase the focus on it to a very intense level.

"At some point it becomes obvious that there is a problem and the first thing that the manager does is try to affix blame."

In crisis management, all the focus, resources, and energy are concentrated on a single priority.

This type of management can be the most rewarding to a person who requires a great deal of control.

Once a group is in crisis management, this person gets a complete reward. When the focus is narrowed to a single priority, a manager gets total control, group communication improves, people feel a great sense of purpose, and most of all, there is a feeling of accomplishment.

People tend to feel a greater sense of positive motivation in a good crisis than in any other period.

Feelings of control, and the rewards of accomplishment may lead a bureaucrat to establish a working environment in which crises are created in order to regain those feelings.

People who work under this type of stress may feel a variety of feelings. If the crisis is real and the crisis process understood, all those involved can feel a great deal of comfort and confidence knowing that the group can perform under pressure, get through a crisis, and learn a lot. After it's over, the entire work group will be better for having performed in crisis. Unfortunately, this is not the normal result of crisis management.

Usually, when the problem starts it is not clear that it is a crisis.

The manager usually denies that there is a problem at all. The workers become aware of the problem but are afraid to tell the boss for fear of reprisal. At some point it becomes obvious that there is a problem and the first thing that the manager does is try to affix blame.

The reason for this is quite simple. When a more senior manager becomes aware of the problem, the bureaucrat must explain it; to save his own position he tries to shift the blame to someone else.

This entire process erodes the group's trust and respect, so that morale and productivity deteriorate.

When denial and blaming finally stop, people turn to action. Total deterioration is at hand and they define the problems, disregard their other priorities, and focus

on solving the crisis.

What intensifies this problem is

"When things go back to normal, life goes back to normal, only with the group more fragmented than before."

that when the crisis is over, the manager becomes aware that during the resolution portion, the work group got something done. There was a sense of purpose, the manager was needed, adrenaline was flowing, and things were very exciting. When things go back to normal, life goes back to normal, only with the group more fragmented than before.

The manager is then confronted with the realization that he or she likes the crisis; he or she might even go so far as to start creating crises – sometimes consciously, sometimes subconsciously – to regain the feelings of control and ownership.

STANDARDS AND PROCEDURES MANAGEMENT

At the other extreme of the functional management continuum is standards and procedures management. In many ways it is a business manager's major task to establish standards and

procedures for the workers and the entire organization to function by. When I think of this type of management I visualize the restaurant business and, in particular, a comparison between a McDonald's and a privately owned restaurant.

When you enter a McDonald's you know exactly what to expect. From the decor to the taste of the coffee, you know what you will get and how much you will pay for it. There will be no surprises.

The McDonald's Corporation has been able to transcend cultural values and international boundaries, using a consistent approach from country to country, culture to culture. It is a continuous management responsibility to train people and focus on the corporation's standards and procedures.

I am often amused when I think that Russian society is learning about standards and procedures from the McDonald's Corporation.

At the other end of the continuum is the private restaurant owner.

When you walk into a neighborhood cafe your

expectations are different. In most instances each visit is a new and sometimes different codes make it virtually impossible to have the standards and procedures change without

"Operational success of any business is dependent upon the ability of managers to maintain consistent and measurable procedures and standards."

experience. Each wait person will act differently, bringing their own personality to the interaction.

The time and the process will vary and the portions served will not always be the same. It is interesting that the vast majority of these ventures fail, while from the first day another McDonald's opens in your neighborhood, it looks as though it's been in business there forever.

It is obvious that in order to be in business and make money you must operate your business in an orderly and consistent manner. Operational success of any business is dependent upon the ability of managers to maintain consistent and measurable procedures and standards.

Successful bureaucrats are responsible for managing these procedures and standards through an unwritten code of execution. These standards, procedures, and the codes to accomplish them become the basis for the culture of the organization. In most organizations the unwritten

highly skilled and mature management.

As in crisis management, certain managers prosper in a highly standardized and procedural environment. It is a very safe and stable environment with a high degree of accountability as to who does what and whose fault it is when things go wrong.

But there is a problem when the overall environment requires a change and the organization refuses to leave the culture supporting the old standards and procedures. The number of managers who thrived in the old environment and stay with the organization is determined by the amount of change required to survive.

ISSUE MANAGEMENT

The third form of functional management is what I call issue management. This type of management is either a skill or happens randomly, depending upon the skill level and maturity of the manager. Whether an organization is in a crisis or running like McDonald's, issues

"In well-running traditional bureaucracies, mid-level warrior bureaucrats give their bosses "heads up" when an issue has left their battleground and is headed up the ladder."

and problems arise that require action.

The style and process by which these issues are handled determine the ownership, the effectiveness, the productivity and the overall morale of the organization. Like the two functional management types discussed earlier, there is a continuum of how issue management is handled.

Throughout this resource guide I offer ideas and techniques to effectively use all three types of management.

The result of each of these discussions will be a combination of relationships and processes that form the unwritten codes of behavior that determine the culture of any given organization.

But the basic idea is that a company's bureaucracy is there to effectively handle issues and problems created in the course of business. Well-run business bureaucracies handle issues successfully.

The major difference in the future will be that the quantity of issues requiring attention will increase to keep up with the incredible increase in the rate of change. In other words, the faster the rate of change, the more issues there will be. Added to this will be a change in the level of knowledge required to make effective decisions.

An organization's ability to handle these high-level issues will determine its ability to succeed.

Typical bureaucratic organizations handle issues mainly through political posturing. In such organizations, warrior bureaucrats look for opportunities to position themselves on any one issue; the politics of the organization determines the outcome. Very seldom do the workers get involved with the process.

Usually, an issue is discovered by a mid-level bureaucrat who informs their boss. The issue goes right to the senior pyramid

head who takes the issue to a rival pyramid head who then works down their pyramid to find out the other side.

These challenges and counter-challenges form the battleground for the political wars of the organization.

In well-running traditional bureaucracies, mid-level warrior bureaucrats give their bosses "heads up" when an issue has left their battleground and is headed up the ladder. *This allows for checkmates and volleys to be played at the point of attack.*

This type of issue management has worked effectively in organizations with large standards and procedures manuals. But the process has created huge inefficiencies and morale problems because it never delivers the optimum answer and seldom involves the people who must continue to work with the issue.

It ultimately causes a certain degree of crisis, putting the organization into an inconsistent environment of high levels of standards and procedures with periodic major crises, a difficult environment at best to work in.

The challenge is to create an atmosphere that allows anyone in the organization to bring issues to the discussion level, allow involved workers and managers to discuss it and then

make a decision that permits it to be integrated into revised standards and procedures.

The key is to let involved and interested people have an opinion on the problem and thoughts about the solution, but not get bogged down in a process that does not allow for timely decisions.

In any organization at any time, all three types of functional management – crisis, standards and procedures, and issue – are being used. I contend that warrior bureaucrats can be trained to operate in all three types, and use these skills to provide a constant challenge for improvement.

The optimal outcome will be an organization that can handle the dichotomy of having a high level of standards and procedures,

with a culture that acknowledges rapid and uncontrollable change as part of doing business.

The Concept of Organizational Change

The only thing we know for certain is that change will be constant. I once thought a great company internal tagline would be, "Change will be constant – so just do it." As the world gets smaller, and the Baby Boomers get older, I can't think of any business that won't have to reposition its company image, corporate culture, or the way it does business.

THE ULTIMATE CHALLENGE OF THE AMERICAN BUSINESS CULTURE IS TO MAKE CHANGE A BASIC CULTURAL VALUE.

This means that an entire organization embraces change as the strength of the company, that the entire employee base, from senior manager to hourly employee, believes that change will be a positive and rewarding experience.

The very idea that a culture could embrace change as a positive is almost too radical to be dealt with.

American business works diligently to produce a standards and procedures environment, to ensure a consistent delivery of goods and services on a daily basis.

The tendency of people who become successful in large companies is to formulate standards and rules to control and conform the workforce. This ensures that change is very difficult, and that the employee has a clear but limited picture of their responsibility in the bureaucracy.

So the ultimate question is, if the goal has been to provide a controlled and procedure-oriented environment, how does the American bureaucracy do a 180-degree change and create one that fosters the level of risk required for the organization to process change? Especially the level of change inevitable in the coming years.

This very question may be the ultimate issue that allows American businesses, the American government, local governments, and the American culture to survive in the future.

There are three ways change can take place. In each case the reason for change is separate from the process that accomplishes the change. But in all cases the manager's abilities and skills determine the pace, receptiveness, attitudes and overall environment.

Whether managed or not, change happens and over time it determines the new culture, the new rules, the new standards. Later on, things will change again and again. People will constantly try to change things for the better, while seeking to minimize change.

THREE WAYS IN WHICH ORGANIZATIONS CHANGE
First Kind of Change

The first kind of organizational change usually starts when organizations hire a manager from the outside because of their experience and technical expertise. These new managers usually come into the organization with ideas, attitudes and experiences that were part of their previous cultures.

After adjusting to their new environment, they may try to implement their picture of how things should run in the new organization, depending on their self-esteem and/or insecurity.

Many times these people leave their past organizations with manuals, forms and position papers in hand. They are confident that it has worked before and will therefore work again. This type of experience is most visible in athletics.

When a team gets a new coach, the culture changes. The team's playing style changes, a percentage of the players changes, and the measure of

success is whether the new coach's style wins or loses more games.

These kinds of business changes don't have as clear a vision of whether or not the change was successful. The style changes, the values change, and in most cases the players change.

The most important skills required to implement this type of change are communication and presentation skills.

The ability to deliver a clear expectation is critical to helping people grasp the new values and define the new procedures and standards.

Success of using outside talent to bring about change is best assured when the bureaucrat hired has direct, day-to-day contact with the area requiring change.

This positioning requires the least amount of management skills because being close to the daily decisions ensures the outside talent is involved in important details, not relying on the interpretation of a subordinate manager.

The higher the level of entry into

a bureaucracy, the greater the need for personal management skills, maturity, and respect to make the change work effectively.

The Second Kind of Change

"If we continue in our current direction we are liable to end up where we are headed."

The second kind of change is less defined and in my observation, more common – with far greater implications for the organization's overall culture.

For some reason, whether from within the company, an outside influence, or the realization that things are simply not working, it is understood that things need to change.

No one knows exactly what should happen, people just know things must change.

The line that comes to mind is, "If we continue in our current direction we are liable to end up where we are headed." In most instances a random periodical change process starts with a series of bureaucratic power plays. In each case the manager sees the opportunity to gain personal power and empire, and the win/lose mentality becomes pronounced.

The resolution of this type of situation is not very predictable or orderly – things just start happening. Eventually, the organization's power structure is realigned. Adjustment does happen, but the human price is very high, and as the pace of change increases, so does the organization's inability to deal with future change.

People take sides, build walls, and become very insecure. This environment creates a great deal of intensity and stress, with people working many extra hours.

Many projects are done twice: First to prepare for the boss's turf battle, then again when the winner has been determined, and the real project has been defined. I believe many American companies are currently involved in this form of change.

They are working very hard without knowing if they are headed in the right direction, and without much hope that their change process is delivering the best answers.

The Third Kind of Change

Finally, I feel this last type of organizational change is required if America's businesses are going to manage their way through the next century and maintain a balance between the human factor and the level of

productivity that is required to succeed.

This change process is a culture of its own – implemented by

"...people who do the work deserve to have some input into the conversation..."

management as an orderly and structured procedure that employees understand and in the end grow to trust. It accepts that the company must experience changes, and it values the fact that the people who do the work deserve to have some input into the conversation before rules and procedures are changed.

I did not say that the people who do the job are the ones who have the best answers and therefore should solve the problem, though they may have many positive insights.

In periods of rapid change, workers will generally lack a broad enough picture to understand the strategic implications of all that is taking place. Therefore, it is very important that the change process accommodate their insights while holding the management team responsible for implementing the decision at the required pace.

As a training director I had the opportunity to facilitate many

"quality circle" groups. The work groups with quality circles did find creative solutions to their problems and morale issues did get better, but the pace of decisions and implementation was too slow for the rate of change in the current American business environment.

For this type of change process to be successful, it must be a combination of attitudes and procedures or techniques that allow a manager from middle to senior management to control the diverse issues confronting the current American business culture.

This process needs to take into account the diverse motivations of the people in the work place, allowing each a structured environment that is understandable, while affording the manager enough control to decide whether or not this level of participation is a waste of time and energy.

I devote the remaining sections of this resource guide to explaining this systematic process for managing a rapidly changing environment.

This also involves convincing the organization that the process is more important than who wins, while allowing the historical bureaucrats to use their hard-won skills in a more harmonious and structured context.

The overall outcome of this management style will allow organizations to manage change, involve people, and still do it at the pace required to survive in the future.

The Architecture of Managing People

All managers and employees become involved in the observation and judgment of people management. In each of my jobs I needed to play two roles at the same time – employee and manager.

The quest to achieve in the corporate structure demanded that the issues of personal accomplishment be tied to my ability to understand my boss's wants and desires. I also needed the ability to interpret those wants to determine which projects were to be accomplished by myself, and which by my subordinates.

Finally, I needed the skills to decide how to best manage and help those assigned to work on those projects. What made all this more difficult was the reality that I had my own agenda of ideas and issues, which I felt were important, and that I knew my subordinates also had ideas,

wants, and wishes that each of them felt were important.

The goal, then, was to convince my boss that I was effective [by getting his list done]; to get my own list done, and to be a good manager by letting my employees grow and work with some independence.

It was obvious to me that without a clear set of management principles – an architectural plan, if you will – there was no way I could consistently get things done. I wouldn't be successful.

From training people, team building, going to seminars, and reading other management books, it seemed that while each system of ideas was useful in some way, none allowed for a reliable philosophy from which to build a consistent management style or approach.

Each represented a technique, a thought, a belief or some knowledge that helped, but didn't explain how all this works. What I needed was a simple and overall plan, philosophy, or blueprint in which I could place all these thoughts and management ideas so that they

would be more effective.

I have concluded that there are four basic principles that serve as the framework for all management concepts and practices. These four principles can be likened to the supporting pillars of a building. They form the basic structure of the overall management process. Once you understand and embrace these principles, you can design and tailor your management concepts and practices in a focused and meaningful way.

PRINCIPLE #1:

Recognize that people will do What they think they ought to do, How they think they ought to do it.

No matter how regimented the task, the human spirit demands personal interpretation. America was built on the concept of "doing it my way." Songs have been written eulogizing the concept of personal choice, our schools preach individualism, our heroes in business are the ones who break out of the pack and distinguish themselves above the crowd.

With all of this emphasis on personal choice it seems ridiculous when a manager wants his or her subordinate to not only do the project, but to do it the same way they would do it themselves.

The fact is that in order to be considered a quality manager, and to get the best results, you need to have individuals embrace, enhance and enlarge any given task or project with their own personal energy and ideas. This individual personal involvement is not only the energy that drives quality working environments, but the basic fuel that takes a project from just being completed to potential group breakthrough.

I have known managers who grumble that they don't want their people to think – they just want them to do what they were told. I submit that this is not possible, that the human spirit requires judgment, interpretation, decisions, and commitment.

The most basic principle of a solid management philosophy is that people will process information, directions, orders, tasks, and issues in light of who they are and their experience.

They will then make judgments on what must be done, and how they feel the project should be completed. It is imperative that

a manager enter all discussions knowing that the individuals involved will interpret the conversation their own way, and choose actions they feel are appropriate.

confronted with success you don't like.

if you are not careful, the next project will have you reverting back to what you will call

"They must know it takes all types of personalities to become a great team..."

This process is the essence of what you want as a manager. Without this principle, a manager is limited by his or her own mediocrity.

"hands-on" management. You will tighten the reins and try to micromanage to ensure your values are not violated, and in turn things will get worse.

PRINCIPLE #2:

Know the values of the people you work with and what they want to accomplish.

Have you ever been involved with a person in a project that was completed successfully, but you didn't like the method by which it was accomplished? For a manager this becomes a true dilemma. The project is completed, your boss said "Good job," but you didn't like the method used.

The hardest concept to deal with, after accepting Principle #1 and designing your management style to use as an asset, is the fact that there is the potential for lots of conflict between people with different values and personal standards. You are now

The critical element in knowing the values of the people you work with is based upon knowing people.

There are many seminars on the subject of personality types: Myers- Briggs and Quadrant management styles (red, blue, green), to name just a few.

All of these seminars enhance your ability to understand yourself as well as other people. I don't know why a manager would be promoted without learning about the personalities and tendencies of other people.

They must know it takes all types of personalities to become a great team – that a work group in which everyone acts and thinks and processes information in

the same manner is doomed to failure. The concept of team in the workplace is the future, as long as it is embraced in a way that enhances and allows the strengths that come from diversity.

Principle #1 must be believed. But knowing about personality styles and motivating, trusting information, processing the information, and then making a decision are only part of the value equation. The other half is all the personal integrity questions: Trust, respect for others, selflessness and showing of ego, and ultimately, self-confidence.

I believe that two thoughts illustrate the majority of the dialogue on these "soft" issues of personal values. The book, *Everything I Need to Know I Learned in Kindergarten*, by Robert Fulghum, is true.

What did preschool and kindergarten teach us?

Sharing, respect for other people's toys and space, letting others finish their sentences, not stealing another person's food, working together to build things.

I think you can tell when someone didn't go to preschool or flunked kindergarten.

As a manager, the hardest issue to deal with is a subordinate who doesn't share your value system. This problem demands that the manager have a clear

understanding of his or her own value system – otherwise there is strong potential for the fight to allow the lowest common denominator to determine the group's value level.

When confronted with a subordinate who does not share your values, you must clearly define which values the subordinate has violated and address only one at a time.

The emotion in this type of conflict can create tremendous stress, because suggesting a person has poor values challenges their very fiber. A personal charge such as this can explode into a nightmare for an organization, but ignoring the issue puts the whole work group in a difficult place. Trust and respect are greatly challenged if differences in values are not properly addressed.

A second thought about people's values concerns an individual's level of self-confidence. It has long been known that people with low self-esteem are more difficult to deal with than those with high self-esteem.

An appropriate level of self-esteem means an individual has utilized his or her past training and experiences well, and understands their significance without allowing the past to preclude future growth. It is important for a person to feel comfortable and confident

making decisions that enhance a project without becoming arrogant and risking its outcome.

It is very important that the manager interview his or her current employees and potential employees with the understanding that once a value problem arises, it is the most difficult management problem to solve.

I always spent a lot of time with my key division subordinates, explaining the reasons for my decisions. I truly believe that over time, when subordinates have an understanding of your values, they tend to adapt these values in making their own decisions.

Once this value consistency is reached, the work group is staged to achieve higher and higher levels of performance because there are greater and greater levels of trust and respect.

PRINCIPLE #3:

Know what success looks like.

The first two principles are more about beliefs and truths than management activities. Principle #3 is the number one management activity. Delivering clear pictures of what success looks like consumes 50% to 60% of your time.

To have people comprehend what success looks like you must understand that they learn in many different ways, and that the process requires a variety of skills that change with the complexity and scope of the picture you are trying to deliver.

This is further complicated by the fact that in some instances, no one really has a clear picture of success; all that is known is that change is required – and no one really knows where it will lead.

In many ways, this statement might best describe America in the '90s: We know that we must change, but what will it look like when we get there? This thought will be the constant companion of American managers for a long time to come.

If all of this is true, then what must be done? Obviously there is no single answer, but a few simple thoughts might clarify this problem and allow the manager to thrive in delivering a clear picture of success.

Thought #1:

A picture of success vs. an objective.

American management and American business schools have decided that if everybody has a clear objective, things will be all right. I believe that this is one of the biggest problems in American management. Management has copped out to a statement of objective and then looked for someone to blame when it didn't work – but

an objective just doesn't do it.

So, management says the objective is to run a 7.5% sales increase, or the objective is to hold expenses to under 32% or to gain a 23% share of the market. Though achieving any of these goals might be considered success, they fail to take into account the fact that human beings make decisions, process information, and communicate this energy to things that have more than one dimension.

They need a picture they can touch, feel, smell, and connect to. It is hard to feel anything about a 7.5% increase because the activities required to achieve it require people to act from a set of decisions, relationships, and activities on a daily basis. People need to see success in its smaller elements while the larger vision is presented as it relates to them personally.

I had the opportunity to attend a five-day facilitator training program presented by Mr. Lou Tice of the Tice Institute. Though Mr. Tice's program has gone up and down in the land of meaningful training programs, his basic premise is correct: You can't accomplish something you haven't decided you want, or can't define in a first person, present tense description.

The use of affirmations has significant merit in the ability of human beings to embrace

a concept, and make decisions and judgments to obtain desired results.

> *Mere objectives will never be enough to make people adopt a clear direction, understand the relationship of the picture to their individual behavior, or allow them to make decisions and judgments with clear and appropriate self-confidence.*

The use of affirmations is much more appropriate; They help individuals understand how the big picture relates to their individual behaviors and responsibilities.

Thought #2:
There is not always a clear picture.
Sometimes, maybe most of the time, there is no clear picture of what success looks like. Something has to change, and there is a general direction in which the group must head, but no one has a complete picture of what it will look like when the group gets there. This is often

the dilemma of the more senior manager.

When I was assigned to run the marketing and sales promotion division of The Bon Marché, I was instructed to bring the company to the next level. Little did I know that five years later, this would include redoing every aspect of the organization: From installing photo studios to developing an electronic publishing system, from changing the creative department to designing and moving into new physical space, from doubling the staff to completely restructuring the staff groups. Throughout all of this, we also established new procedures for deciding what was to be produced, and how to do it.

The process of this transition became more important than the picture – because it was the process that developed the picture. The point was, though I could not share a real clear picture of what the division would look like when we were finished, everybody seemed to know when the process was complete. When there is not a clear picture, there must be a clear and well-understood process.

All subordinates must understand how the process works and how they are to be involved. The process replaces the picture, and as the employees adopt it, the group still gains most of the same benefits of having a clearly defined picture.

I discuss different types of process management in the Types of Management section.

Thought #3:

People learn and connect to thoughts and concepts in different ways.

With all of the energy being directed toward education, learning styles, right brain/left brain functions, management styles, learning disorders, etc., it seems obvious to me that though the concept of delivering a clear picture of success is relatively simple, the skill required to be effective is more complex. While there is no simple checklist of activities, there are a few basic standards you must deal with.

Gary's Code: The key to understanding is in the detail, and the detail is the written word.

Whatever the learning style of the people you work with, a short, concise written document is a must. First, at least 50% of the people need to read a concept or idea in order to give it quality reflection.

There is one thought that permeates successful strategy. The thought is that in a competitive world the person with the best, most well thought-out plan wins. A

"Managers cannot spend too much time clarifying the picture of success..."

written document that describes the overall objective – **Who, What, When, Where, Why** and **How** – allows everyone who must deal with the plan to not only understand, but add key thoughts and ideas.

You can write your ideas down in detail, explain to people one at a time what you want, and hold group meetings to ensure the group knows what you want. But no matter how much the time you spend doing these things, it is still highly possible that the picture and the detail will not be clear.

Managers cannot spend too much time clarifying the picture of success and discussing the details of that picture with their subordinates.

Spending a long time in the discussion of what success looks like, I submit that as a manager and as an employee, there is no concept more important to understand.

PRINCIPLE #4:

Give people resources and get out of their way.

This is where concepts such as the "one-minute manager," servitude management, and the art of delegation all fit. You see people decide what they should do, related to their specific job and tasks, and they choose how to get it done. Now it is your job to get the needed resources for your people and let them do their job.

How many times has a well-conceived plan been managed to death by a manager who could not let go?

You must be attentive and present to ensure ongoing clarification of the picture. It will always need discussion, but you can't micromanage your subordinates or they will make no personal commitment to the project.

As a manager, I no longer necessarily have the fun of doing projects. To deal with that problem, I keep some projects for myself, and don't allow anyone else to manage them. I get involved with all aspects and

everybody knows that these are my projects.

Instead of micromanaging other people's projects, I micromanage my own. This allows me to stay very busy and excited about my job and my own learning curve, and lets my subordinates have the trust and respect that must be given if you truly believe Principle #1.

At the opening of this section, I wrote that all the seminars, books, courses, and principles of management are important and have merit, but that I personally needed a framework within which to place those concepts in order to better understand, and, in turn, use them.

I truly believe that this blueprint of management allows for the overall framework within which many of these concepts can be used.

Defining a Corporate Culture

Creating sustainable, high-performance, working cultures in today's business environment is a primary focus of all major corporations.

With a highly-competitive marketplace, adjusting to the increasing level of global competition, creating environments that are capable of out-performing competition, accepting a rapid pace of change, and creating fresh and new ways of moving forward are cultural traits that are in high demand.

So, how are these high-performance cultures created? What does it take?

I believe that the first step in creating a sustainable, high-performance culture is being able to define the culture that exists in terms of behaviors and practices that can be adjusted, changed or added on.

There are specific areas of discovery that will define the essential ingredients in the creation of a sustainable high-performance culture. Once a

culture is defined, then it can be adjusted.

The five key indicators that can be assessed to build a sustainable, high-performance culture are:

1. Operational Leadership
2. Directional Leadership
3. Deadlines
4. Employee Reward Programs
5. Internal Employee Communication

Focused, edited, and directed culture development begins and ends with leadership. Leadership starts at the very top of the organization and eventually becomes an issue at all levels, including the individual who holds no title but, through personality, holds a position of power and influence in a specific area of the organization.

The ability for leaders to make decisions as to what is important vs. what is less important is a critical thinking skill. All tasks and projects are not equal, and timing of when to do what is very important.

The biggest problem in the development of a high-performance culture is having too many things that are all too important.

Great leadership understands there are things that need to be done regularly to manage the operation efficiently and effectively, but these activities only keep you where you are. They don't move you anywhere.

In order to move the organization or team forward, a leader must balance those things that must be done regularly with key initiatives that are directional and strategic in moving the group forward.

The ability to edit what is not useful and focus on key activities at the right time in the business year are the critical leadership qualities that create a high-performance culture.

So, how do you know where you are?

OPERATIONAL LEADERSHIP

The management of the current operation is the first task of leadership. The operation is managed through three primary tools:

Key Reports:

Great leadership relies on a selected set of key reports that help focus the organization on the critical operational issues of the business.

How to Assess

Ask several layers of leadership what their top five reports are – reports that are used at least once a week.

Ask each individual what information he or she is looking for, and what decisions are made by looking at these reports.

Outcome

The organization's operational focus will be determined by the consistency of the answers. In high-performance cultures, all levels of management review a basic set of reports and take consistent action from the information.

Key Management Questions

Much of what happens in a culture is determined by what questions are routinely asked of people in the organization. If a question is asked over and over, the people who are asked only have three options:

- Find the right answer to the questions
- Leave the organization
- Answer the question wrong and eventually get fired

The power is in the questions!

How to Assess

Ask several layers of leadership to define the top five questions that are asked and to define the answer people are looking for.

Determine the consistency of what people believe those questions and answers are.

The power is in the questions!

Outcome

Companies that have a high degree of consistency in knowing what the top questions are will have a more focused approach to operating the company.

Operating a company requires a degree of consistency in the managing of the operation. This level of consistency comes from the focused and edited use of reports and key management questions. The more consistently the leadership talks about these elements, the greater the chance that the organization is focused on managing the operation.

Meetings

Understanding where and how meetings are held gives insight as to what kind of leadership is in the organization.

How to Assess

- Are (all, most, some, none) important operational meetings held in the senior management work area?
- Are (all, most, some, none) important operational meetings held in the operations area of the company?
- Are there regularly scheduled operational meetings?

- Do operational meetings have a (fixed or variable) agenda?
- Are issues and problems discussed openly in operational meetings?
- On a scale of 1-7 (1=low, 7=high), how often do the operational meetings feel like they are dealing with a crisis?
- On a scale of 1-7 (1=low, 7=high), how boring are the meetings?

The answers to these questions will give you insight on what type of interaction takes place around the operation of the business.

Outcome

Strong operational organizations have defined operational meetings with a predictable pattern of interaction and involvement. Issues are openly discussed and dealt with. Crisis discussions are saved for when there is a real crisis.

DIRECTIONAL LEADERSHIP

The second and equally important function of leadership is leading or directing the organization toward the future. In America, you cannot stay where you are. You are either moving ahead or going backward – you never stay the same. Leaders are the people who are keepers of direction.

I am not going to discuss how leaders choose a direction – there are many ways. I would hope that the organization has a strong sense of its identity or brand, and that the leaders use this sense of identity to focus and enhance the organizational direction. I will discuss performance cultures and the practical aspects of the organization's ability to move forward and change.

The key element to a business culture's sense of direction is what I call key initiatives. A key initiative is an activity that happens in conjunction with managing the operation. These activities usually require more than two major corporate functions to work together to accomplish the project, e.g., marketing and operations.

Generally, there is a need to communicate the nature of the key initiative and its activities to the entire organization. The initiatives are clearly different than just managing the business. Many times the expense to execute these initiatives is separated from the normal budgeting process.

How to Assess

After describing the key initiatives concept and its differences to operational management, ask these questions:

- What are the key initiatives that the organization is currently engaged in?

- How many of these initiatives happen yearly?
- Describe when you know you have been successful in instituting a key initiative.
- Do you have (too many, not enough, or just right amount of) key initiatives?
- How do you fund your key initiatives – from your budget or with separate funding?
- What type of meetings do you use to manage these key initiatives?
- Describe how different levels of employees add input into what or how key initiatives are executed.

Again, the consistency of answers to these questions will demonstrate the level of focus senior leadership is capable of providing. High-performance cultures have clearly defined processes for managing key initiatives.

Outcome

People know their roles and they clearly understand what needs to be done and how to do it. They are allowed to enhance the plan and take ownership of the projects required for successful completion of the initiatives.

The critical issue to great leadership is the understanding of how much direction the people of an organization can

manage. To quote a famous song, "you need to know when to hold them, know when to fold them – and know when to walk away..."

Great leadership knows when to focus on improving operations and when to add key initiatives to move the organization forward.

DEADLINES

A great deal of intelligence about what type of culture a company has will be determined by understanding the nature of the deadlines the company and its employees face. Not only will you be able to understand the culture, I believe you will be able to predict the personality of the individuals who will be attracted to and promoted within the culture.

I believe you will also be able to predict the nature of the cultural shortfalls that will keep the organization from sustaining a high-performance culture.

Deadlines are those moments in time where something must be produced and there's a ramification to be dealt with.

In my consulting work around companies' brand identities, I have become aware of the power of deadlines. When a company has a significant level of deadlines, the nature of the culture becomes very task-oriented.

Decisions need to be made, and process falls victim to the deadlines. These types of cultures regularly have individuals feeling disassociated from the organization. The employees often complain about not being asked before being told what to do.

The people promoted most often are those who are ready to take charge and get things done. These take-charge people are rewarded for getting things done and taking no prisoners.

In cultures that do not have a high level of deadlines, the opposite happens. Things tend to be processed, sometimes to death. There is a need to get lots of people included and people making quick decisions are often considered pushy, not team players.

Neither of these two extremes creates the best high-performance culture. Both types of skills – decisive decisions and adequate process – are required to create a sustainable high-performance environment. The question is how do you discover what the organization currently acts like?

How to Assess

Asking leaders about the quantity and intensity of the deadlines their company faces will offer great insight into the nature of the existing culture:

- Describe the type of deadlines the company faces.
- Describe the type of deadlines your division or team faces.
- When a deadline is not met, what happens?
- Does senior management allow enough time for employee input into how a decision is made?
- Does the organization seem like it has a lot of crisis just prior to a deadline?

Outcome

Companies that have lots of deadlines can also have enough process to engage the employees in a meaningful discussion of what the best course of action is. In these environments ownership of the outcomes will be spread to a variety of levels of the organization.

If there is too much process with no decisions, or too many decisions with no process, the organization will develop a sense of frustration and ownership will be held only by a few

senior managers. A committed workforce will be hard to develop.

EMPLOYEE REWARD PROGRAMS

In all business cultures, people are rewarded. These rewards are in the form of titles, more interesting work projects, invitations to key social functions, relationships with senior managers, recognition through formal rewards and, of course, more salary.

> *When an individual is rewarded, everyone in the organization is put on notice about how to act.*

Also, once an individual is rewarded, the entire organization judges the fairness of the reward system. This judgment goes much deeper than just formal rewards. The entire review process also plays directly into the employees' judgment about fairness in the organization.

In many companies, reward programs are part of a competitive climate that senior management feels is healthy. The employee with the most sales wins, or the one with the best quarterly production numbers.

Most of these rewards are tied to short-term results and in each case, as the culture develops, other employees form opinions about what is really important and how fair the company is.

Rewards go a long way in creating an organizational culture. Be careful who you reward – they are the winners and everyone else is a loser.

How to Assess

Through a series of one-on-one interviews with different levels of the organization, you can determine a great deal about what is highly rewarded:

- Does the company have a formal reward program? Describe it.
- Does everyone in the company have an equal opportunity to be rewarded?
- Do the same people always seem to be rewarded?
- Does the company have any rewards for teams of people?
- How are rewards given out?
- Do you care if you receive a reward?
- Outside of the formal reward program, describe other ways you have seen people rewarded.

Outcome

An organization's reward program will help determine what type of culture the organization has. The key to

rewards are: Do they build a sense of common focus or create individual competitions between coworkers? Do the reward programs help build a sense of fairness or do favorite people seem to always win? A sustainable, high-performance culture will have people wanting to be rewarded for outstanding performance.

INTERNAL EMPLOYEE COMMUNICATION

Internal communications are the fuel for a high-performance culture. People who are informed feel they are trusted and respected. Kept in the dark, employees gossip and create their own truths. "Who knew what when" becomes a source of power in the organization.

Creating a sense of community that shares information across all levels of the company helps develop the openness required for solving problems and issues at the lowest level possible. When employees are treated only with a need-to-know attitude, there is a sense that they are not important in the process. Lack of ownership occurs in these types of cultures.

How to Assess

In a series of one-on-one interviews, a great deal of intelligence about an organization's communication patterns can be gained:

- How do you find out about important decisions that have been made?

- Is there a lot of discussion in the back hall about what people think is happening?

- Does the company regularly send newsletters or emails out to all employees?

- Do these corporate communications talk about tough issues that the company is facing?

- Do you value the information that is provided in these formal communication pieces?

- Who do you trust to give you the best information about what or how the company is doing?

- Does your boss answer your questions about what is happening in the company?

- Are employees asked for input that has an impact on how the company operates?

Outcome

Organizational cultures that have clear and open communication with their employees will build a greater sense of common purpose than those that don't. High-performance cultures live on open communication.

CONCLUSION

There are five key indicators that can be assessed to determine the fundamental building blocks of a sustainable,

high-performance culture:
*Operational Leadership,
Directional Leadership, Deadlines,
Reward Programs, and Internal
Communication.*

All play important roles in
the company's organizational
culture. Taking an assessment
of these cultural building blocks
on a regular basis will give you
a better understanding of what
dynamics are creating the way
your employees are engaged in
making a difference.

Employees who understand what
is important, who are challenged
to improve how things are done,
who are engaged in enough
process yet take deadlines
seriously, and who feel informed
and trusted in knowing what is
going on, will take ownership in
helping create outcomes that
sustain high performance.

Leadership and Values

The successful manager in
today's climate needs a
number of tools in order to
stay a key player in a traditional
organization. The same is
true for a leader in the new
environment and culture of
companies that survive in our
future fast-paced working world.

> *There is a great deal of
> risk in creating a new
> style and culture in
> American business.*

Though many attitudinal changes
are taking place every day, the
reality is that many American

> *"They need to deliver
> the results of the
> old culture while
> embracing a longer
> term vision and
> attitude..."*

managers got their positions the
old-fashioned way: By winning in
the old culture.

They must continue to look, act
and survive in that culture while
intuitively believing in a different
one. This means their own
organization may experience a
different culture than the rest of
the company.

They need to deliver the
results of the old culture while
embracing a longer term vision
and attitude than many of
their peers. This whole process
requires a sense of purpose and
a belief that there is a better
way.

I previously mentioned that one
of the two major reasons for the
rapid change in the business

environment is the Baby Boom and its effects on all aspects of society.

I have a general belief that buried in the front edge of the Baby Boom is a group of managers who were permanently influenced by the '60s experience.

These people are just hitting their 60s, and taking their place in the senior executive ranks of many businesses. They have quietly been working their way up the corporate ladder, investing in their families and their careers, and are now going to be placed into key decision areas at a critical time in American business history.

These same people were attending colleges and universities when major American institutions were not accepted as truthful and changes were being demanded. They questioned the values of the leaders, and without any vested ownership, forced change in the system.

Today these people do have a vested ownership in a system, but are being confronted with the prospect of needing to change – the very thing they demanded in their youth. The definition of the values they hold dear will be questioned. The spirit of the '70s and early '80s is deep and I project that it will play

a role in the coming years.

The desires to change, to work toward a greater good, and to be more involved in important decisions, along with a greater commitment to the human spirit, will pay a critical role in America's ability to manage its way back to economic power.

THOUGHTS ON VALUES

This guide contains many references to values and their role. Most employee problems are related to a difference in values. In a business environment your values are reflected in three distinct kinds of decisions: How you spend money, how you use your time, and how you treat other people:

HOW YOU SPEND MONEY

Every manager has some power over spending money, whether personally or by their people. No matter how many times I have discussed spending money, the conversations are the same:

- How do you relate to the cheapest price?

- What do the words "best value" mean?

- What is the role of loyalty and quality service?

- What are the factors that allow you to trust someone?

If you share similar views on these topics with others, there is a strong chance you will spend money the same way.

The problem with spending money is the fact that most major corporations struggle to increase profit margins in very competitive environments. This leads to very short-term decisions in order to "make the numbers." This truly puts the long-term/short-term goals and decisions at very intense points, when the result of the discussion is the awarding of contracts or choice of a producer.

HOW YOU SPEND YOUR TIME

Use of time seems to be most tied to personality styles. Each manager spends a majority of his or her personal time either at work or thinking about work.

This equation is somewhat based on the manager's commitment to the company's plans and strategies, fear about job security, or the manager's workload.

> *The problem with judging people's use of time is you never know whether someone is just spending time or is being productive.*

In many ways, quality time is related to clear priorities and the level of focus that an individual is able to maintain.

As the old story goes, when alligators are biting at your heels, it is difficult to remember that the reason you were in the swamp was to drain it – even if you have gotten rid of some of the alligators and only the new ones are left.

The reality is that managers are judged by their boss as to whether or not they are efficiently using their time; at the same time, each middle manager is judging their subordinates' use of time. In the end, judgment is related to the level of a shared focus and picture of what success looks like between each manager, their subordinates, and the boss.

HOW YOU TREAT PEOPLE

The most telling value, as well as the area of management relationships with the most

> *"Self-centered people will always start with a 'me first' attitude."*

potential difficulty, is the perception of how you treat coworkers. People feel strongly about the treatment of other human beings. In many ways, the degree of a person's self-centeredness becomes obvious when it comes to how they relate to others.

Self-centered people will always start with a "me first" attitude. The simple signals of letting someone else speak without

interruption, and making sure everybody gets a chance to participate seem basic, but in stressful and aggressive environments they are the true test of an individual's values in this area.

Everything you really needed to be successful you learned by the time you left kindergarten. And though many times the class bully got his way, we all know that in the end the class bullies failed. People got faster or bigger, or more likely smarter, and at the right time the bullies were "had."

Even in the most aggressive environments, people who treat others in a respectful manner are given extra support when they are in trouble.

People who become the organizational bullies always get helped "out" whenever they run into trouble. The payoff for treating people fairly is when you are in trouble other people will try to help you. If you are a bully, don't mess up or you're dead.

Always ask, am I leaving this person a way out with dignity?

- If the answer is yes, other people will notice, and trust and respect will grow
- If the answer is no, watch out!

Loyalty Requires a Culture Built on Continuous Feedback.

The world has changed and this statement rings true.

The question is, how do you Do a culture built on continuous feedback if you have never experienced this type of culture in the past?

Does this just sound like an out-of-control level of feedback that makes getting anything done impossible? Or can an organization use this type of culture as the edge to not only create greater loyalty, but to also create an operating model that is faster to change, makes less operational mistakes, and responds to the current economic environment in a timely manner?

This transformation is happening. It is being accomplished for very little expense and, in most cases, over the long-run it will reduce marketing and communications costs, training costs, and employee turnover. It creates a working environment that responds effectively to all types of challenges without creating a crisis.

As if trying to create an internal culture built on continuous feedback was not important enough, with the rise of social media and networking systems, you are now confronted with the fact that your business is already being discussed and judged online.

As our environment becomes more and more connected – Google, Amazon, Craigslist, Yelp – everywhere you look, consumers are rating products and telling their experiences about buying and using your products.

DEVELOPING A CULTURE BUILT ON CONTINUOUS FEEDBACK

Changing Your Basic Approach

STEP 1: DO BEHAVIORS FOLLOW ATTITUDES OR DO ATTITUDES FOLLOW BEHAVIORS?

As Americans, we have developed the art of presentation – or selling. People get ideas and they learn to be successful by becoming great presenters, and becoming experts in using PowerPoint. Just think of those two words: Power. Point. – not much listening or dialog in that concept.

In the '80s, for four and a half years I was the training director for a regional department store (The Bon Marché). I had two major challenges:

1. Change the selling culture from a clerk environment to that of a professional customer service selling culture, involving 40+ stores and over 5,000 salespeople.

2. Create a greater sense of teamwork in each of the operating units.

These two great projects were accomplished with the management concepts of the 1980s and no email technology.

THE CUSTOMER SERVICE EFFORT.

As in the 1970s and 1980s, there are six ways a retail store can differentiate or position itself – price, value, quality, selection, service, and cool.

It wasn't until Nordstrom got a major amount of press on its return policy (the story of how Nordstrom took back car tires) that the nation started paying attention to customer service.

The book was called, *The Nordstrom Way*. It was with this new awareness about the loyalty factor of customer service that the retailers, and eventually all organizations, became engaged in adding customer service to their management focus.

So, there I was, given the challenge to take the local department store [located across the street from Nordstrom] into the customer service world.

The Bon Marché had been the value department store and our company tagline was "Where the Choices Are" – which meant the company was focused on value and selection, and now we were going to add service.

"...in the world of retail, company policies and the managers' behaviors and level of focus have major impacts on workplace attitudes."

The chairman of the company had an experience that put him on the path to change the company's service culture. He had gotten sick while traveling to New York City - and, not having anyone with him, there he was - sick and alone.

He went to the hotel store to purchase some aspirin. The young employee noticed he was sick and took it upon herself to check in on him several times a day for the next few days.

This became the chairman's favorite story and, during the four years of this service effort,

he told it whenever he could. He called this, "Customer Service From the Heart," and it was the passion that drove the decision to enter the new world of customer service.

"Customer Service From the Heart" is about an attitude. Asking 5,000 salespeople to have this attitude was a great starting point – but, in the world of retail, company policies and the managers' behaviors and level of focus have major impacts on workplace attitudes.

The first thing that had to change was the company's return policy. To return something to The Bon Marché in 1983, a sales associate would have to get a department manager to sign the return credit and then the customer would have to walk to the cash office to get his or her money back.

So much for customer service and good attitudes.

On top of this return policy, the company had a very strong "security" attitude – which meant the inventory was closely checked at least two times per year and departments that had excess inventory shrinkage would be given extra management oversight.

Again, not good for customer service or service attitudes.

So, this "protect the merchandise" and "make it hard to return" mindset was a problem for "Customer Service

From the Heart." How could you compete with Nordstrom [which took back car tires] when our customers had to go to the cash office with two signatures to get their money back?

This became the birth of the "I Guarantee It" cultural change. First, every salesperson now would have the power to take back the merchandise, and

"...you are now an associate, and each of you has the power to deal with your customers without a management signature."

we changed our "clerk" title to "associate." So, all of a sudden, we told the organization it was "Customer Service From the Heart," you are now an associate, and each of you has the power to deal with your customers without a management signature.

Wow! What a shift – and, for the first nine months no one believed it was true. There were still inventories and security and, while a few wanted to believe, there was a wait-and-see approach – "I don't want to be the first to screw up."

As we messaged, trained, and met with teams of employees, we also decided that we needed a Mystery Shopper Program, which we called "The Hanger Report." It was an opportunity to design a survey and then

pay a "professional" shopper to come into each of our stores and give a rating for that shopping experience.

Although mystery shoppers are still relevant and used in retail today, this started as a total disaster. Stores would get between four and 12 mystery shops per month and, although the shops were random, the ratings would always include the date, time of day, and department shopped.

So, when the scores came out, it was obvious to store management which sales associates had received the

"...we just found another way to pressure and make the associate's job more difficult."

bad scores – and, of course, the department manager used this to tell those associates about the score.

Now the entire store looked at these shops as just another typical management hammer – we didn't trust them – we just found another way to pressure and make their jobs more difficult.

So, here we were trying to drive "Customer Service From

the Heart," and our mystery shoppers were showing our associates that we had no heart, we just had mystery shoppers.

Well, one morning I got an idea that turned out to be one of the lessons that I still use today – and is the most important foundational element of any cultural change.

Management needs to transfer the ownership of the change to the employees. Until they own it, it is just another "best practice" [or, as we used to say, a BOHICA – or "bend over, here it comes again"].

The idea was to have all 5,000 employees take our Mystery Shop Survey and go shop a store of their choice, and rate that store's service on our standard. I had thought that the real problem with our effort was the fact that the associates really did not know our standards or expected behaviors. Instead of more training classes, I wanted to have them experience the shop from the customer's point of view.

You can imagine the reaction I got when I presented this idea to my boss (the senior vice president of human resources). But, to my amazement, a week later he said it was approved.

We would give all employees [ncluding sales associates, the distribution center, the corporate offices, and the chairman] one hour to go shop a competitor. then hold a meeting to discuss their experience and report to their boss.

The results of this all-company activity were incredible. Not only did every employee gain an understanding of our service/ behavior standards, almost like magic the company got PRIDE.

You see, they found out that we were better than most other retailers – and, in fact, if you went to Nordstrom and were not "dressed right," you were ignored. Nordstrom people are paid on commission, so if you "look right" you get lots of attention, if you "look wrong" and you are ignored.

The attitude changed when the entire company understood the behaviors of our customer service expectation, and decided to not only own those standards but believe we were better than the competitors.

There was also another lesson that now is even more important: As frontline employees held meetings to discuss their experience, the managers were put in a place where they had to listen. In

many cases, the associates were given their first opportunity to give input about how to improve the service.

What a concept – our management team listening to the employees and receiving quality input on how to make things better.

Four Great Lessons Came From This Experience:

1. Cultures don't change until the people in the culture own the change.
2. It's all about behaviors.
3. Pride is required to have passion.
4. If you want to get better, management needs to listen.

So, we spend a lot of time figuring out how to change cultures and improve attitudes.

How do we compete in this new world?

When it is all said and done, these four lessons may say it all.

STEP 2: IS IT ALL ABOUT THE LEADER OR ALL ABOUT THE TEAM?

The Softer Side of Management Training

Throughout my entire career, I have always been interested in the role of management in creating and sustaining organizational cultures.

As is always stated, the culture of an organization begins at the top and its impact on the entire organization is substantial.

What the senior leader pays attention to, the questions they ask regularly, whether they are seen outside of their "power place," if they seem to like people, who gets promoted, and if they seem to know what they are talking about – all have a huge impact on how the organizational culture develops.

At the time I was given the challenge to change the customer service culture of The Bon Marché, I was also asked to improve our management training program – and to especially focus on the organization of our stores. Again, this was the mid-1980s and the hot books were all about the softer side of management – people skills.

Management is always about getting/delivering numbers – top-line sales, margins, efficiency – all focused on delivering bottom-line profit.

In the 1980s, we were still in a period where, although quarterly

reports were important, American companies focused more on annual performance.

So, there I was, looking at a 40-store department store chain with a highly developed operations culture, trying to bring on a customer service enhanced culture, with store managers who were not always the warmest/kindest people in the world.

The culture that got them promoted wanted quantitative results. The company would always do its planning by establishing the profit margin it wanted, projecting the top-line sales, and then put all of the operating expenses into the middle.

In other words, since store labor was the largest expense category, the company's business operating strategies always added up with the final decisions being made around the expense associated with people – the number of people, production per hour, full-time vs. part-time – all of those business decisions that create human resource issues. In those days, department stores were open seven days a week, up to 12 hours per day, and this always meant lots of people with lots of personal issues.

There, in the middle of the 1980s, we were changing cultures, adding customer service, improving attitudes, improving profits, and trying to change how management worked together.

THE EFFORT OF TEAM BUILDING

The common leadership and management philosophy was: We need better teams and more management self-esteem. We all had distinct personalities and, based upon the work of Carl Jung, everyone was learning their Myers-Briggs personality profile, or their red/blue/green management profile, or the Quadrant Personality [where you are a controller, persuader, amiable, or analyzer].

What were your strengths and weaknesses? Could you learn to understand your impact on other people with different styles? Could you as a manager understand that great teams had a diversity of personalities, and it was NOT a good thing to only hire and work with people like you? And, because of the way the historical retail culture was managed and rewarded, was the store manager really the king?

In the '60s and '70s, stores were very independent and, as long as they made their numbers, were left alone. But starting in the late '70s and throughout the early '80s things had changed. More corporate oversight came to be the norm.

Of all the store team-building seminars I did, I will never forget Bellingham. You see, Bellingham had always been a very independent branch store. A new store manager had just replaced a man who had run the store for over 40 years. And, of course the younger aggressive "I like my new power" store manager had the store in a state of crisis. If that wasn't enough, a brand new mall had just opened four miles up the road and we now had two stores in the city – the old downtown store and the store in the new mall.

I had developed a two-day program that was designed to help bring 10-25 people together [the normal size of our store management teams] to learn some personal growth, stress-coping, and team goal setting skills which, along with the new effort at enhancing our customer service, would work together to increase the company's sales and profits.

Paul, the new store manager, had been counseled several times that he was being perceived as too forceful and judgmental, and did not give his managers any say in their work.

As usual, the first day was almost totally devoted to having people discuss their personality patterns – were they forceful and goal-driven, were they very analytical [requiring them to think before they acted], were they very amiable [always hoping to help others just get along], or were they persuaders [selling, selling, selling and having a good time]?

The management group was similar to almost all of our stores – the store manager was a controller, the financial person was an analyzer, and the rest of the team were persuaders or amiable – all struggling to understand all of these changes.

After people did their profiles, the first day of the seminar was always the best. In many cases, this information was very powerful. Often, this was the first time in people's lives they could understand how and why they felt the way they did, made decisions the way they did, and got frustrated at other team members the way they did.

As was normally case, by the first afternoon I would have a room of people working in the same building, working for the same company, discussing the different ways their relationships were working. If it was going well, we would start to discuss how things might improve if they used this information.

It was in this situation that my most interesting discussion of all these efforts happened. You see, Paul was an off-the-charts controller and, although he could understand what was going on, he had no interest in changing. In fact, he became more

convinced that if there were just more people like him, things would be better.

The idea in those days was to try to change people's attitudes, which would improve their behaviors, and one of results would be "Customer Service From the Heart." If you had the right attitude, behaviors would follow – the same held true for team building.

As I have reflected on this experience, and view the total work of those years using the best thoughts of the decade, I am struck with the idea that, in both my customer service and team-building efforts [give people empathy, that we are all different and we need to understand ourselves, we need to understand how our styles impact others, and with the right attitude], I believed that teams would get better.

Well, Paul didn't even pay lip service to these concepts. As I think back on the impact I had on all of these organizations – people did have personal breakthroughs, but I don't believe they were sustained because the goal of the seminars was to focus on attitudes not behaviors.

As with the summary of my efforts with improving customer service, cultures do not change until people in the culture own the change.

- It's all about behaviors
- Pride is required to have passion
- If you want to get better, management needs to value listening

THE CUSTOMER LOYALTY EXPERIENCE SYSTEM

The Customer Loyalty Experience System is a comprehensive approach based on aligning all behavioral aspects of the organization's culture toward a consistent and engaged customer experience. This is achieved by effectively receiving, managing, and responding to continuous customer and employee feedback.

The quality of the customer experience is vastly improved, the level of employee ownership is greatly enhanced, customers and employees have a greater sense of pride in the organization, and the organization is able to respond and change much faster – giving it a significant competitive advantage at surviving and thriving in our current business environment.

How Does This System Work?

All great systems work because they are easy to understand, easy to execute, and it's easy to determine how they are working or measure the results.

I have two recent experiences which, coupled with my work in

the 1980s ["Customer Service From the Heart" and team building], help to confirm the idea that *"Behaviors don't follow attitudes, attitudes follow behaviors"* – and it's just not that complicated.

EXPERIENCE #1

Virginia Mason – Helping to Redo a Medical Clinic

I was asked by my personal physician if I would participate in a one-week brainstorm to help totally rework a Virginia Mason Medical Clinic. Because the Kirkland clinic was moving to a new location, there was an opportunity to radically reorganize the way the clinic worked.

Virginia Mason had a very large investment in looking at their business [a hospital and 12-15 clinics] through the eyes of the Toyota Production Management method to re-engineer the way the medical clinic operated: lean, efficient, and very user driven.

We started this one-week brainstorm with an end in mind – greater efficiency for everyone, including the doctors, nurses, specialists, and last [but that is what I was there for], the customer. In the end, it was an amazing week. For five days, 25 people – doctors, nurses, clinic manager, architects, everyone in the business – went through this very formal process to:

- Cut the number of steps a doctor and nurse walk by 50%

- Manage the supply of all the medical things needed to do their work with a just-in-time approach

- Let the patients become a bigger part of the system

The basic tool to design the space was a concept they called the "Fish," which was really just a process of engagement – thinking through a transaction and defining all of the steps that the patient needed to take and matching those transaction points with what the clinic employees had to do.

In this diagram, there are two sides – the patient [customer] and the organization. The steps involved for each side are listed, to examine efficiencies.

For example:

Patients have to park, so the clinic had to think about what getting into the parking lot was like, and how big the stalls should be for their patients, and how older people get out of their cars and get into clinic, etc.

The next transaction interaction was checking in – what does the patient do and what could be done to ensure that when they showed up, this step could be more efficient? When the appointment reminder call was made, what could be done to

ensure the visit went well – to be both efficient and create an outstanding experience.

Every process in the patient's visit, every process in the clinic business operation went through a "Fish" process. Notes were kept, priorities were established, and policies, procedures and behaviors were defined.

The Virginia Mason Kirkland Clinic opened in March 2009, and it is starting to do most everything it set out to do with regard to improving efficiency.

As expected, some of the older patients are having some trouble. One of the changes was to eliminate clinic waiting rooms – efficiency means no waiting. As the patient representative, I was not old enough to realize that older patients often go to their medical clinics weekly – and they like to talk to other weekly clinic visitors. Oh well, so much for efficiency.

Learning #1
You can look at any operational transaction and create a "Fish" approach to understanding what behaviors, policies and procedures must go right every time for the user to have an outstanding experience.

Learning #2
You can have your employees and customers involved in defining the "Fish" and add real insight and valuable consciousness to how things should work more efficiently, and how to create a dynamic and measurable experience for the user.

Learning #3
This process transfers ownership to the employees – they become vested in not only how it should work, but also as the behaviors become the work standard, the organization has employees that champion the cultural change. Management is listening to the employees and customers before they try to change the culture. Attitude follows ownership of the behaviors.

EXPERIENCE #2
Tully's Coffee – Where I Got to Test my Long-time Belief
I had been the head of Alumni Relations for the University of Washington for over five years and it was a wonderful experience. During the last year and a half at the UW, I was asked to join the Tully's Coffee Board because of my retail background. Ultimately, I left the university to become CEO of Tully's.

Tully's is a coffee company that roasts, wholesales, and retails [at the time] in over 90 stores in six states, and provides office coffee through distributors. The company had about 900 employees, most working at the

retail stores.

There are lots of learnings from Tully's, but this story is about "clarity, alignment, and passion": How do you change a culture, grow the business, and create a store environment that results in loyal customers?

So, as a management person, the ramifications of this compartmentalized analysis of the job performance, was that the whole thing became political – one person's opinion vs. another person's opinion.

I decided that I wanted to try

"How do you change a culture, grow the business, and create a store environment that results in loyal customers?"

Almost everything needed to be redone – stores, chairs, tables, refrigeration, employee benefits, management culture, products [not the coffee], and most of all, the customer service culture.

One of the major shifts we made in our hiring practices had to do with a personal long-time frustration: We hired people by first writing a job description and then selected a person to do the job.

Once you were hired to do that job, you were told that you would be reviewed – and in almost every case, the review covered different expectations than the job description. So, we hired you for one thing and we reviewed you for something else.

In the service business, it got worse – we had some form of customer/shopper review that, in most cases, was again different from the job description and the performance review.

something I had always thought would work – write the job description so that a manager could review their team on what they were hired for.

And then I got lucky! In walked Max Israel and his product, Customerville. Customerville is a 24/7 behavioral feedback system where the customer scores their view of behaviors that must go right every time for the customer experience to be great.

Customerville also allows the customer to give comments to the company and, if the comment is bad, it instantly sends a text message to a management person. If the comment is very positive, management can print a customer-gram to give to the employee or team of employees.

So here was the perfect integrated system. You write the job description based on behaviors, make those behaviors a central part of the review

forms, and let the customers rate those behaviors as well.

What an amazing outcome:

1. There was clarity. These are the behaviors that must go right every time, and you get continuous feedback on how the team of employees is doing.

2. The company was asking for comments and, in today's world, customers have comments. If it was a bad experience, the manager got to go for an instant recovery, and if it was good, the employee or team received recognition.

3. Politics disappeared. It no longer was just a bunch of discussions about what I thought vs. what you thought. Now it was what the customer thought.

4. Teamwork – no longer did the worst performing employee define what management would tolerate. Now the employee team pulled the poor attitudes/performance up or forced them out. It was the store team's scores, not a manager's opinion. Teamwork comes from team members, it does not come from management.

A THOUGHT ABOUT RECEIVING CUSTOMER COMMENTS

I can easily tell if an organization really wants to hear from its customers. I just look at how deep into a company's website I have to go before I find out how to contact the company. As soon as I find the "contact us," I look at how I get to do this. In most cases, it's just an email address or they give you a list of all the senior executives.

Having access to the senior executives is much better than just an email address, but this means that the senior executive is the one who holds the power – in almost all cases, these comments are about something bad.

Just think of the power of using "tell us what you think" or "we would love your feedback" as something that is at the top of the website. It is promoted as a primary message in all of the company's communication. What if customers actually liked giving you ideas and ways to improve your business? What if your business was driven by customers who "believed" they were part of the team?

This is very powerful stuff. "Word of mouth" is and always has been the best way to grow your business. What better way to grow your business, than to get customers involved?

The customers become your eyes and help find the best new products, better policies, and a more efficient operation. And, in today's world of social media and social networking, your company

embraces this engaged culture, instead of ignoring it or hiding from it.

Developing Loyalty Requires a Culture Built on Continuous Feedback

CONCLUSION

At the beginning of this section, I asked the question: If you have never experienced this type of

> *"...by effectively receiving, managing, and responding to continuous customer and employee feedback, the quality of the customer experience is vastly improved."*

culture, can it be created or is this just an out-of-control level of feedback that makes getting anything done impossible?

Well, my answer is that building a continuous feedback culture is very straightforward, and will produce better results on both the top line [sales], as well as on the bottom line [expense control]. Here is a brief summary of those 10 steps:

1. Make a conscious decision that you are going to develop a culture that is built on listening, not telling.

2. Take every transaction between customers and employees and do a "Fish" that helps clarify those key behaviors that must go right every time.

3. Redo your job descriptions and make sure all employees have defined behaviors that must go right to provide outstanding customer experiences.

4. Redo your review system to include those critical behaviors as something that managers and employees talk about at least two times a year.

5. Develop the right questions that will provide a 24/7 feedback and a customer comment system to make sure employees get direct behavioral feedback weekly on these critical behaviors.

6. Move "we want your feedback" to the top of the communication and marketing efforts. Drive the customer to engage with your business.

7. Make sure the survey reports reports and customer comments are a weekly part of your key management meetings.

8. Make sure everyone knows that you are paying lots of attention to this program.

9. Continuously ask your employees if they have any ideas that would help improve the business.

10. Be liberal with your team praise – make sure doing well at the most things is rewarded.

My four great learnings from past experience are:

1. Cultures don't change until the people own the change.

2. It is all about behaviors.

3. Pride is required to have passion.

4. If you want to get better, management needs to learn to listen.

Introducing the Customer Loyalty Experience System:

A comprehensive approach based on aligning all behavioral aspects of an organization culture toward a consistent and engaged customer experience. By effectively receiving, managing, and responding to continuous customer and employee feedback, the quality of the customer experience is vastly improved.

What Successful Management Looks Like

It seems that for the last few decades, the focus in the business world has been to limit the human factor. Workers are thought to cause too many problems – it would be better if all business functions were handled by robots and computers.

This is simply not true. The only way organizations will be able to survive the future shock of a rapidly changing environment is to let the human factor process and create the solutions. The human factor is the difference, and we must, as a management group, acknowledge this fact and take on the challenge of developing the management mentality and skills required to set the human factor free.

This task will require a major reculturation of the political bureaucratic organization.

As organizations change and prosper because of this reculturation, other companies will embrace these attitudes and values – or fail. The future is now.

I will now attempt to define the culture and practical relationships of an organization that understands how the continuum of "types of management" is used. It's an environment with a high degree of standards and procedures, that is also able to handle unpredictable crises and a constant flow of issues needing resolution in order for the business to survive during a time of rapid change.

HIGH-STANDARDS MANAGEMENT?

The basic type of management of any organization is a high level of standards and procedures that govern the consistency with which the organization treats its reason for being. If it's a sales organization or a production organization, it is critical that these be understood and carried out within very tight guidelines of performance.

If the organization does not have a written base – if these standards and procedures are only communicated orally – the organization is, or will be, in serious trouble. Like the McDonald's Corporation, the ability to make money on a continuous basis relates directly to the level of order and consistency the organization can deliver.

If a company is small, unwritten standards can be communicated and levels of success can be achieved, but the organization will reach the wall and start failing as soon as it outgrows the level it can manage in an informal manner. The entire organizational structure and the job descriptions are totally dependent upon strong standards and procedures.

The key to this type of management is two-fold: 1) Training and communication to ensure all workers share the same understanding, and 2) Each employee taking ownership of the standards and procedures.

This type of management requires that the bureaucrat be trained in communication skills and that he or she constantly reviews and refers to the appropriate procedures and standards. There is usually an audit to ensure that actual performance is matching the established standards on an onging basis.

Companies that effectively have this environment are described as being strong operational companies. Many times you will hear people talking about the bureaucrats as quality operators. These companies understand procedures.

The standards are high and for one reason or another the workers understand and execute consistency. *This is the basic level of operation that allows the making of money.*

If the organization doesn't make money, it means that either the standards and procedures are not good enough, or the workers don't understand or are not executing to the standards.

In the best case, the organization respects the company's standards, understands its procedures, and makes money as a result. The employees feel ownership and audits are viewed as checkpoints, not as witch hunts.

CRISIS MANAGEMENT

The second type of management needed is crisis management. In a well-managed company there are very few crises because problems are identified before they reach that point. But on occasion some outside or internal force creates a crisis.

A crisis can happen in an individual area or to the company as a whole.

No matter what the crisis, well-managed companies handle the process in the same way; once the crisis is identified, the steps are the same.

The senior manager identifies a crisis without first looking for blame. The primary belief is that the crisis needs to be resolved and who did what can be discussed much later.

"Companies that effectively have this environment are described as being strong operational companies."

The most important concept is to manage the crisis to a positive conclusion.

All involved parties are gathered to discuss the crisis, the potential outcomes, and the effects they might have on the organization or team. The group identifies its best plan and sets about the execution, making it a very high priority. Other parts of the business may suffer; other tasks may not be accomplished.

Generally, one person is more affected than the others, so there is a great deal of satisfaction knowing that the team members are supporting each other in the time of crisis.

Upon completion or gaining control of the situation, there is respectful discussion of how the crisis started, and what needs to happen in the future to ensure it doesn't occur again.

In some cases, standards and procedures are rewritten to help ensure that what is learned is incorporated into the business environment.

In the best case, all levels of the organization learn something and the company feels a sense of accomplishment and community for surviving together. The feeling that the sum of the parts is greater than the individuals is reinforced.

ISSUE MANAGEMENT

The third type of management is the heartbeat of a strong and thriving bureaucratic organization – issue management. The true test of an effective and respectful bureaucracy is that any person in the organization can raise an issue without fear, and that the culture of the organization can embrace the issue, discuss it, and feel that it will be resolved without people having to defend their territories or justify their existence.

With a strong issue management culture in place, when a change is required, the organization knows how to respond, and lives in the secure faith that things are constantly going to get better.

The keys to an issue management culture are a strong, mature, and trained management, a clear and well-understood corporate mission, and a secure workforce with high self-esteem.

With these ingredients in place, issues created by the need to change and get better are handled efficiently and effectively, with the organization able to embrace the change with enough speed to capture an ever-increasing level of momentum.

The critical formula is that any individual can and should identify key issues; anybody affected by the issue has the right to be informed and participate in the discussion, with the most senior manager ultimately making a decision.

In addition, group problem-solving must be tempered with a global perspective in order to ensure the issue is resolved with the big picture in mind. It is very important that the workers feel they have a voice in the discussion, but they do not always need to win.

Any organization with a management team that understands how to establish an effective, positive standards and procedures environment, that can handle a crisis without first fixing blame, while encouraging a constant process of finding ways to improve the business, will be better able to handle any change in the business environment of the future. With this environment firmly in place, an organization will constantly focus on improving performance.

I like to tell the following story when explaining how to know if your organization has arrived at this point:

In 1984 I opened a restaurant called Treats, which lasted for four years and was under constant change. Treats had a full menu, gourmet ice cream, fresh bakery goods, and lots of coffee, especially espresso.

For the first two years, our employee conversations about success were devoted to things like making sure the proper bakery sign was with the right baked goods (cookie sign with cookies, for instance).

By the hand sink next to the espresso machine we had a white hand towel that became very dirty after a few coffee spills. Success was keeping a clean towel in front of the customers.

Near the end of the second year I noticed that our picture of success had changed to a discussion of how to make a beautiful latte. You see, we used glass latte cups, and if you steam the milk first and then pour the espresso into the hot steamed milk, there is a marvelous layering of color – dark brown at the top to light brown in the middle to white at the bottom.

With a light sprinkling of chocolate flakes on the top, we had the prettiest latte in town. Now the significance of this story is two-fold:

1. A latte costing $2.40, which looked like what I have just described, cost us no more than one priced for $1.75 that was just mixed together. The customer liked to pay $2.40 for the pretty one.

2. The story became my people knowing when we were getting close to success.
   When our discussion became focused on the little things, the enhancements, the fine tuning, we knew we were getting close.

Cheers.

The Nature of Passive Resistance

The most significant element in the success or failure of any group of any size, from a small business to a country, is the level of passive resistance present in the environment.

In the book, *The Machine That Changed the World*, by James P. Womack, there is a discussion of workers in a mass production environment withholding knowledge and effort from the process as a result of the mass production system.

We need to acknowledge that the individual employee can no longer be separated from the success equation.

All employees, hourly or salaried, must focus together, share a common concept, and each – in their way – add value to the project.

In my opinion, one of the key indicators of a company's quality and its ability to survive and prosper in the coming years will be the level of passive resistance in the organization. Said in the opposite way, I believe the key indicators of a company's quality, and prediction of its future success, is the level of employee commitment toward focused company goals.

Passive resistance is the lack of action or lack of commitment that employees express when they feel disenfranchised from the overall company or its decision-making process. It is also possible for people to totally support the company yet be passively resistant to an individual superior. This is a critical problem if multiple groups must work together to achieve success.

If a company needs a major change to ensure survival, the level of passive resistance may be the determining factor in the survival equation.

The human spirit is the company spirit, organizations have hearts and souls, they are families. People spend the majority of their lives within the confines of the work environment. A broken spirit equals a broken organization.

Passive resistance takes many forms. Its basics are that of withholding information and effort, but the impact is much greater in an environment needing change. Though information and effort are passive resistance's major costs, the real price is in new and fresh ideas or ideas held as a chip in the poker game to ensure a

person's self-interest.

Passive resistance breeds a

> *"...a company that has engaged its employees will have a much greater chance of survival and success..."*

community spirit of mistrust; it creates cliques and animosity. It enlarges turf wars and puts people into an environment constantly looking for flaws in other people. It tears at the foundation of all positive human behavior.

If passive resistance is allowed to continue, a company that must compete will fail – unless its competitors suffer from the same problem. In contrast, a company that has engaged its employees will have a much greater chance of survival and success, even if it is not competitive in all other areas.

I had a discussion recently about whether a company's workforce is a fixed or variable expense. During hard times, does an organization keep a full workforce or just pare back the number of employees to the level required to return to profitability?

Many large firms in the U.S. have been confronted with this problem. I believe that the larger the layoff, the more passive resistance has been present in the organization.

Lean and committed organizations do not over-employ; they do not layer with over-activity. They can't. The employee's commitment doesn't allow this to happen. The test to determine the level of passive resistance in any organization, large or small, is simply the difficulty the organization has in making changes.

> *The simple answer to fixing passive resistance is engaging the employee. The words are easy. The process involves a total change in the American manager's belief systems.*

Protecting the Empire

In all types of bureaucracies, one of the major jobs of any bureaucrat is to protect the empire. To an even greater extent, the goal is to conquer and acquire other people's empires. In many big companies this activity becomes the major focus of all levels of the organization.

Fortunately for the organization as a whole, one of the side benefits of this empire building is business performance. The fact that in the end, a company's business performance determines the ability of the current managers to stay in power, allows better performers to ultimately gain more of the empire.

But generally, empire building is not accomplished through efficient and profitable business. In large companies it most likely has to do with information, communication, and the control of relationships between people who need to know and people who would like to control who knows.

All organizations have seven types of power bases. To list these powers in any order of their overall importance would be a mistake. The type of power that is most important is somewhat dependent on the nature of the organization, the stage of business cycle it is in, and the way each form of power is used.

The overall concept of power determines the size of the empire. The lines of the empire can be visual, as in organization charts, as well as invisible, as in informal relationships.

But in all cases they are real, and the quest to protect one's empire or to enlarge it is the basic element for the soap operatic quality of a business culture.

THE 7 POWER BASES

1. **The Power of the Title:** In most bureaucratic organizations powerful people have powerful titles. The titles are generally earned through the use of one of the other forms of power.

2. **The Power of Association:** In all organizations, who-likes-who has a heavy influence on which jobs and tasks people are assigned, as well as the overall opportunities one receives.

3. **The Power of Technical Knowledge:** People with the greatest amount of technical knowledge always find a way to exert power, although it is often limited to their area of technical knowledge, unless accompanied by another form of power.

4. **The Power of the Size of the Budget:** In many instances the size of the budget determines the level of influence one has.

5. **The Power of Personality:** Each personality has its moments. Our innate strengths serve us well when needed. In most instances people put themselves into environments where their personalities are best suited.

6. **The Power of Age and Experience:** Older, more experienced managers have seen more, been burned more, and can use lines like, "I have seen this before."

7. **The Power of Wisdom:** A few people are unusually wise, with the ability to make great judgment calls or deliver golden statements of truth in important settings.

No matter which form of power or combination of power is used, the ultimate use is to maintain or increase one's empire.

There is an old adage in large bureaucracies that everybody is replaceable.

There are lots of young and eager fast trackers waiting in line to replace tired bureaucrats who are no longer willing to play the game. In fact, one of the spoils of being a strong power player is the ability to deliver titles to subordinates in greater quantity than those in rival pyramids.

Every day, people come to work fighting small battles that determine the landscape of the empires.

Since budgets are never able to accommodate all parties to their complete satisfaction, many of the battles revolve around spending, and who gets to say yes – but the more interesting battles usually deal with who knows what and when. The ability to know something someone else doesn't allows for posturing, and maintains a person's ability to remain on top.

The overriding reality of all of the empire building is control. People who thrive in historical bureaucracies are generally control freaks.

Having control is sometimes more important than making good decisions.

The Power of a Clear Vision

What is Vision?

How do you create a vision?

How do you transfer a vision to others?

Webster's Ninth New Collegiate Dictionary defines vision as:

- **The act or power of imagination**
- **Something seen as a dream, trance or ecstasy**
- **Mode of seeing or conceiving**

In the mid-1980s, I was given the chance to be the director of training and communications for the regional department store, The Bon Marché.

This was a wonderful experience that gave me the challenge of changing the service culture for over 5,000 employees. Part of the challenge of this effort was to take a large group of employees and engage them in owning a new standard of behaviors that were in many ways totally different from the behaviors practiced in the history of the operation.

In researching different ways of trying to accomplish this, I was encouraged to attend several seminars that dealt with the concepts of how to change people's behaviors and attitudes.

The seminar that dealt most with vision was presented by Lou Tice and the Pacific Institute. I completed the five-day seminar and received my certificate as an official Pacific Institute facilitator, which allowed me to purchase the program materials and facilitate the presentation of these materials to Bon Marché employees.

"...until you can see what you want, it is impossible for you to get it."

The basic message of this program had been given to Nordstrom employees, and Nordstrom was now leading the nation in selling customer service as a core business factor. The Pacific Institute materials were considered the gold standard in enabling Nordstrom employees to embrace this level of behavior.

What I discovered was not that the program sold a service concept. No, the Institute's program was built around the concept that until you can see what you want, it is impossible for you to get it.

If you can't see it, you can't get it!

What an interesting concept. Once you are looking to buy a brick home, all you see are brick

homes. Until you decide you want a deck on your house, you don't see lumberyards. Until

"...the majority of people are tangible – they see things as they are, not as they might be."

you see yourself as a great sales associate, you can't be a great sale associate.

So, the great driver of any organization is not that is has a great vision, it is that the great vision is owned by the individuals who need to see the vision, in order for the organization to accomplish that vision.

<u>Here is the dilemma:</u> *Vision is intuitive and inspirational, and the majority of people are tangible – they see things as they are, not as they might be.*

Being visionary is great, but transferring a vision to others represents brilliance. In functional management, there are three distinctive parts to a management system:

1. Crisis Management
2. Operational Management
3. Initiative Management

To think that one vision works for all of these management needs is wrong. In many ways you need to define a vision for each of these management functions.

LET'S START WITH CRISIS MANAGEMENT

If you have read other sections of this guide, you know that I don't believe that managing a crisis is a vision unto itself. The vision for a crisis is that people do not panic and they all have an image/idea of how it will be handled.

This concept of how to handle a crisis is that the crisis is the exception to the rule, not the rule itself. [I do believe that there is a group of managers who find a crisis in almost everything they do. If you are working in an organization where senior leadership needs a lot of control, there is a chance there will be more crises than needed – just as a way to allow the senior management to have a sense of greater control.]

In a true crisis everyone should know what to do, and that requires the foresight to envision what should happen.

OPERATIONAL MANAGEMENT

Operational management vision sometimes looks more like a series of objectives connected together.

In my view, the operational vision is more associated with

the organizational culture and should support the organization's brand.

So, I have now introduced the concept that vision, culture, and brand are all associated with each other. The relationship of these three elements becomes very intuitive and inspirational – but they all are interrelated. Each has to be connected for the organization to maximize its human capital.

There are many tools that support this vision area, including:

- Job descriptions
- Performance standards
- Employee surveys
- Dashboards
- Reward programs
- Employee reviews

This is best summed up in the statement: "This is how we do things."

INITIATIVE MANAGEMENT

In initiative management, vision is everything. The concept of change and finding creative solutions, no matter where your organization is in its life cycle, means you will have to change what you are doing or you will have to change how you are doing it – the speed at which change is happening is mind-altering.

There is a chance that you don't actually have a clear vision or picture of where you need to go. Then the process and analysis of developing brand culture helps to clarify vision and build ownership.

The core issue is still the ability for everyone in the organization to share ownership and clear understanding of the process of:

- What is going to change?
- Why this change/initiative is necessary?
- How will this process get us there?

The language of this vision area is:

- Initiatives
- Cultural change
- Business development
- Aspiration

All of these concepts are leveraged with organizational risk and reward. Though the vision offers a picture of success, the outcome is up to the execution, and the employees' responsiveness and effort to get there. If the employees do not see and understand the picture of success or the process that is happening, you will fail.

If you can't see it, you can't get it!

So how do you transfer ownership of a vision?

My answer to this question is very old school. I think business

leaders have lost the power of the old school approach to managing their cultures.

After the last nine years of financial stress, the response of leadership has primarily been to downsize below the level of logical employee needs, focus on quarterly profits at the expense of long-term vision, and, in some cases, focus on just plain greed.

We have lost the time required to ensure that organizational vision in all three areas of operations can be communicated and supported.

The organizational infrastructure has been neglected, and the possible ramifications are serious and sad. Having said that, I believe that reinvigorating the basic old school approach does not require excessive time or money, it simply requires seeing how – if done in alignment –the outcome will be very rewarding.

In basic communications training there are two sides to any communication:

- **The sending of a message**
- **The receiving of the message**

It is the sender's responsibility to send a clear message, and in a perfect world, the message receiver is responsible for receiving the message and verifying what was communicated.

If the sender does not trust that the message is being received, then the sender becomes responsible for establishing mutual understanding. In other words, it is management's responsibility to make sure that employees "get it."

In my consulting work, I listen for two statements that give me a clear picture of how a culture is doing:

- "I thought we talked about this"
- "I wasn't trained that way"

These two phrases clearly demonstrate that the organizational vision has not been communicated to the level of understanding required for organizational success.

Alignment of the basics is the easiest and quickest way to transfer vision, focus an organization, and align vision, culture and brand into employee behaviors that maximize an organization's human capital return on investment.

WHAT NEEDS TO BE ALIGNED

It starts with a strategic plan [not a five-year plan, but a plan for 2-3 years]. In addition:

- Job descriptions that support the plan
- Hire criteria the supports the job descriptions
- Policies that enable success

- Training programs
- Internal and external messaging
- Dashboards that demonstrate progress
- Quality assurance reviews
- Annual reviews that relate to the job descriptions and strategic plan
- Reward programs that relentlessly focus on the things that are going right
- Employee fun

Winners Celebrate – Losers Retreat.

A QUICK STORY TO END THIS SECTION:

I recently returned from a trip back home to Omaha to visit my family and friends. As a Seattleite I always prefer to fly Alaska Airlines, because they now have a direct flight. But they also offer many other behaviors that distinguish their employee team and contractors from all the other airlines that I have flown.

I arrived at the airport over an hour ahead and I did not have an assigned seat for my return flight, so I went to customer service. The agent saw that I was tall, and without asking, thought to assign me an exit row seat.

I dropped my bag at the bag drop before boarding, and the baggage attendant smiled at me and explained where I would get the bag when we landed.

The flight attendant was a friendly greeter, and throughout the trip both attendants were very present, walking regularly up the aisle, asking if we needed anything and picking up waste. The attendants were very focused on recycling the waste and they were thanking everyone for their help, as we all tried to separate our waste.

They announced a credit card promotion with not only bonus points, but also a companion reward program for your annual anniversary. When we got to the end of the flight, the captain wished us goodbye, and my checked bag got to luggage pickup in fewer than 15 minutes.

It was a very pleasant experience – I don't know about you, but pleasant has not been a word I use much for flying in airplanes these days.

Alaska's human capital sees the vision and demonstrates the power of how that vision drives culture and fulfills on their brand. *I think they do it the old fashion way – and it seems to work.*

WHAT DRIVES VISION? [A Survey]

- Vision takes the right people who can debate vigorously in search of the best answers, yet people unify behind decisions regardless of parochial interests.

  Circle 1 2 3 4 5

- Leadership is about vision, but leadership is equally about creating a climate where the truth is heard and the brutal facts confronted. There is a huge difference between the opportunity to "have your say" and the opportunity to be heard.

  Circle 1 2 3 4 5

Creating a climate where the truth is heard involves:

- Lead with questions not answers.

  Cirlce 1 2 3 4 5

- Engage in dialogue and debate, not coercion.

  Circle 1 2 3 4 5

- Conduct autopsies without blame.

  Circle 1 2 3 4 5

- Build a red flag system to ensure truth is not ignored.
-
  Circle 1 2 3 4 5

- Vision is not a goal to be best, a strategy to be best, an intention to be best, or a plan to be best. It is the understanding of what you can be best at. The distinction is absolutely crucial.

  Circle 1 2 3 4 5

- Vision is best created and supported by people who display extreme diligence and stunning intensity [they rinse their cottage cheese].

  Circle 1 2 3 4 5

- Vision is driven from the inside. When it is understood, transitions feel more like an organic development process.

  Circle 1 2 3 4 5

- Vision requires patience and discipline. It follows the "build-up-break-through" flywheel model despite pressures to achieve faster results.

  Circle 1 2 3 4 5

- Vision needs to have incredible commitment and alignment, which guides transitions and changes organically.
  Circle 1 2 3 4 5

- Enduring visions preserve their core values and purpose while their business strategies and operating practices endlessly adapt to a changing world.
  Circle 1 2 3 4 5

SIX WAYS TO BE IN ALIGNMENT WITH A VISION

1. **People:**

   The right people, the right values, the right position, in the right place. Who gets promoted, who gets fired.

2. **Measurement:**

   What you measure is what you focus on.

3. **Communication:**

   All types all the time, both ways; always saying the same thing.

4. **Powerful Catalytic Mechanism:**

   What demonstrates your vision?

5. **Super Consistency:**

   Everyone goes out of their way to ensure we are consistent.

6. **The Flywheel Effect:**

   It's not the short term but the persistence to build to last, as the best. Results grow and grow.

Thoughts About Communication

In many ways all of what I'm talking about is communication. Communication is:

- What you say
- How you say it
- What you don't say
- How you don't say it
- What you look like
- How you react
- How you don't react
- Your values
- Your ability to anticipate what people are thinking or feeling

It is about *being*. You might say that the holistic approach to any human relationship is communication.

What I like most about being a

> **"The question, "I thought we talked about this" are the proof of poor communication."**

manager is taking accountability for becoming a quality communicator. It is a never-ending process and challenge.

I live by a simple three-step view:

1. If you and I have a discussion and fail to communicate, I am responsible. It is easy to know when we have failed to communicate.

The words, "I thought we talked about this" are proof of poor communication.

I recognize that communication is a very difficult and time-consuming skill, and that I should not change my opinion or actions toward you if this is our first miscommunication – but I will double my efforts the next time we communicate.

2. The second time we misunderstand one another, we must recognize that we are starting to form a habit.

At this point we must have a serious conversation about what we are doing to create miscommunication, because the next miscommunication will be the third one and there is something about repeating a problem for the third time that is serious.

3. In baseball you strike out and go back to the dugout. The third out means that your team gives up the bat. Third-time criminal offenders are locked up for a long time. We must respect that three times makes a habit and we all know that habits are very hard to break.

As a good communicator, you have to take responsibility for your role in the communication process. If you are the sender, then it is your responsibility

to send a clear message or picture of what you want to communicate. As the receiver, it is your responsibility to make sure you have clarified the message, or reached mutual understanding.

> *If, as the sender, you don't trust that your message has been received, then you must take on the task of ensuring mutual understanding.*

This usually takes the form of a question: Asking the receiver what they think they heard and what actions they plan to take.

If you have had a miscommunication with someone it may be very important to become more assertive, and take on the accountability for gaining mutual understanding.

The process of quality communication is about trust. You can't trust someone you can't communicate with – the only thing you end up trusting is the fact that you can't trust them. Once this happens, no further communication will take place.

We spend a great deal of time talking to people, trying to inform, sell, direct, or convince them of our opinions and thoughts. We do this because we live in a very verbal society.

It seems to me that most Americans are extroverted; if they are typical, they first think of themselves, and how they might make their best impression or how they might feel most comfortable. But being a great communicator requires you to spend more time thinking about who is going to receive your message, and the best way for them to understand it.

A few rare people are able to simply ask questions and through this probing approach, have the other person discover their message. I suggest that this is the most powerful method of developing clear communication, because it utilizes communication's most basic truth: It's not as important what *you* think you said as what *they* think you said.

People act according to their own perception of truth, not yours.

Presentations are a very important means of corporate communication. The truth is that opinions about people's quality and ability are disproportionately related to their presentation skills. Somebody who looks good and acts comfortable in front of crowds and delivers a quality presentation is usually thought of more highly than someone

who doesn't.

A quality presentation is based on only a couple of very basic rules:

1. Know what you are talking about. Knowledgeable people always have the best chance of knowing the right answers and things to say.

2. The second rule is even more basic than knowledge of the subject: Tell them what you are going to tell them, tell them, and then tell them what you told them. The purpose is to inform or convince somebody of something and make sure they don't miss it.

> ## *The most valuable skill I learned in graduate school was the ability to generate a brief written communication.*

I was taught that if an idea is worth talking about, I should be able to write a simple, 1-2 page document explaining:

- The objective
- Who will be involved
- When it should take place
- What the project should be called
- Where I expect it to happen.
- A rough idea of how I think it might be accomplished

I have found that at least 50% of the population doesn't really want to discuss an idea; they prefer to read about it, then spend private time thinking and reflecting on it, then providing quality comments. Bureaucratic documentation is also very valuable; every document should be dated so people know whose idea it was and when it was presented.

All of this is important, but the real importance lies in getting things done in organizations, as well as taking quality communication seriously. Once you have talked about an idea you may still not be sure what other people's opinions are, and you will certainly be wondering if you have approval to continue executing your ideas.

The written document gives you the highest probability of success. It is a formal proposal that can be passed on or left behind after a conversation. It can be presented without a conversation and it serves to ensure that people are informed of actions expected to be accomplished. But most of all it demands response.

Let's look at possible outcomes:

A person may say they agree with what is written, and that serves as an immediate okay.

In another instance, they may

not say anything, but you can start on the project knowing that you informed them and that they had a chance to object.

A third possibility is that they don't like the idea and let you know. That gives you the opportunity to find a strategy to overcome their objection.

Finally, they may tell you that your idea seems okay, but they would like you to change a certain part of it. This lets you start the project, and increases their commitment to it. In many cases, their suggestion may actually prevent failure of the project.

I strongly suggest that if you can't write a one-page document on the basic questions, you don't have enough knowledge or commitment to the project to be talking about it in the first place.

Finally, I'd like to talk briefly about building intuitive communication with somebody, and the incredibly positive effect it has on the level of trust and respect between people and groups.

Intuitive communication is when you almost don't need to say anything to someone and they know what you're thinking. It's what people hope to have with someone they choose to live with. It's the most powerful dimension in any kind of relationship.

We are all looking to belong. We want to be accepted and trusted, committed to a cause and to goals that we can share in-depth with other people.

We are hired by companies and not given the opportunity to choose our coworkers, yet we seek this depth of relationship.

So how do you as a manager create an environment that fosters communication, is intuitive, and builds trust and respect?

Well, much of this work is about the processes and skills required to create this environment. I don't believe in a basic $X + Y =$ intuitive communication formula. It's accomplished day by day, project by project, crisis by crisis, and success by success.

The most important part is starting with great human empathy. That means accepting that others will see the world based upon their view of it, not yours. People need to know what you do, what you know, what your values are.

They need to know they can talk about these things – that you have made this a priority. As a

manager, you can work very hard at being a quality communicator, and create an environment and communication standards that help promote trust and respect. You can let people know they belong by the way you treat them.

These are the basics of an atmosphere and professional culture that gives people the best chance of developing intuitive, communicative relationships.

Creating a Message System That Builds the Brand

Why is a message system important?

Brands are built on having employees and clients talk about a company using the same words and phrases. The stories that are told about the company bring these words and phrases alive and in doing so, create a truth about the organization.

The brand then becomes a self-defining reality with a culture building around the vision, ensuring the brand is nurtured, supported and sustained.

A strong brand will enable an organization to foster employee and customer loyalty, and this loyalty will grow the business in two very powerful ways:

1. Through return visits and stable employment.

2. The fact that both employees and customers share a strong sense of pride, which is needed to establish and sustain an intense passion for the organization.

Loyalty is built on creating pride and passion in individuals, both inside and outside of the organization.

A passion for a brand is the pathway to building a reputation, and a powerful reputation is the key to having employees and customers help build and grow the business. This system will build an intellectual connection to the organization, but more importantly, it will enable an emotional connection – which is the fuel of loyalty.

THERE ARE FOUR LEVELS OF A MESSAGE SYSTEM:

1. A list of key words.

2. Phrases that are easy to remember and emphasize the brand.

3. Stories that bring the concepts to life.

4. An effective descriptor phrase or tagline.

The following is a draft of a project I did with a financial services company – that I hope demonstrates the power of a message system:

TAGLINE CHOICES

This must work for all business units:

- Built on Integrity, Grown on Trust
- Our Commitment, Building Your Trust
- Financial Solutions for a Complicated World

All of the business units share three brand tenants. This system allows for additional tenants to be created, which support a business unit's specific needs. For example, Equity Capital Markets needs to be known for its research leadership.

All units share the following three tenants:

- Outstanding Financial Professionals
- Passion for Performance
- Outstanding Client Service

IT'S ALL ABOUT OUR REPUTATION. This is a

statement defining an image of the culture of the organization. We are a firm that values human capital on a personal and professional level– our clients, our people. We empower employees to do what's right for our staff and clients.

We have a collaborative spirit and inspire fun at every opportunity. We are proud to work with talented people who are obsessed with performance and who always put their clients first.

"You are known for the people you keep."

Key words:

- Honest
- Collaborative
- Independent
- Trustworthy
- Integrity
- Insightful
- Experienced
- Loyal
- Smart
- Knowledgeable
- Successful
- Flexible
- Personal
- Fun to be around
- Leaders
- Long-term focused
- Performance focused
- Processes that work
- A culture that supports work-life balance

Key Phrases:

- The business was built on smart, market-knowledgeable people
- We are research driven and client focused
- We are the best in the verticals we own

- We have industry knowledge, but are regionally based
- We are regionally based, but nationally regarded
- We tell clients what we really think
- We grow the right way
- We live on square deals
- We know that clients vote with their dollars
- Our references are solid

Key Stories:

"Our senior management is very accessible via phone, email, as well as in person – they make an effort to visit the branches and hold open meetings to employees. We all get a personal email for our birthdays, as well as any noteworthy occasion. Senior leadership was just here and after the branch meeting asked for the client associates to stay behind – he wanted to provide us with a forum to voice our opinions independently of the FCs."

"We have always been impressed with how senior management actually knows who we are and our spouse's names also. They really show they care. My regional is the best I have ever worked for, and I have worked for a lot in my 31 years as a manager."

"Our Chief Market Strategist bought dinner for a client of mine after a seminar and visited with her for two hours about her portfolio."

"You are known for the accountability you have had."

Key Words:

- Research driven
- 80 years of success
- Profitable
- Stable
- Active, not passive
- Successful
- Smart investing
- Maximizing value
- Partnerships
- Taking the long view
- Financially conservative
- Customized solutions
- Research drives active financial management
- Personality and reputation of the analysts
- Investment ideas [thought leaders in our areas of expertise]
- Industry knowledge [best in channel]

Key Phrases:

- We are the best in the verticals we own
- We have industry knowledge, but are regionally based
- We are regionally based, but nationally regarded
- We tell clients what we really

think

- We grow the right way
- We live on square deals
- We know that clients vote with their dollars
- Our references are solid

Key Stories

"At a recent business cocktail party [current and former board members of a small private school], an attorney I know asked where I worked. When he learned where, he was very complimentary of the Compliance Officer, based on several communications he had with her involving a mutual client [I believe it involved an estate settlement or similar issue]. He described that she was friendly, professional, and thorough. I was very proud and impressed that she had made such a positive impression."

"You are known for the way you focus on your clients."
Key Words:

- Client always come first
- We are proactive
- Accountable
- We go beyond
- Hard work
- Tough hours
- We empower people to do the right thing
- Responsive follow-up
- We take a long-term

approach

- We customize solutions
- We solve our client problems
- We help our clients understand
- We don't buy trust, we earn it
- Focused on building trust
- We explain and educate well
- Our goal is to actually know our clients
- Treating clients as if they were your family
- Listen more than talk
- Transparent and frequent communications with our customers
- We deliver thoughtful, honest, and unfiltered advice
- We try to make a difference not just be a salesman

Key Phrases:

- We listen more than we talk
- It is about dialogue, not monologue
- We deal with one relationship at a time
- We ask the hard questions to help clients navigate their life journey, whatever that entails
- We offer a personalized approach to meet clients' financial needs and the depth of services and products required to meet those needs
- We have the freedom to do

the right thing for our clients

- We put clients first
- We are a company that asks one question to be successful: "Is this in the customer's interest?"
- We customize our financial solutions

Key Stories:

"There is a story of an elderly gentleman who was very concerned after he was informed of the IT security breach – He arrived unannounced and the Chairman spent two hours letting the person discuss his feelings and thoughts."

"You are known for the financial insights you describe."

Key Words:

- Have channel checks
- Relationships with the buy side
- Have great industry contacts
- Industry knowledge [best in channel]
- Knowing the clients and them feeling confident in the advice
- Research drives active financial management
- Ability to maximize value for the client
- Longevity in the business
- Known for accurate and fast execution

- Great to work with
- Easy to work with
- Having the right product
- Personality
- Best price and likeability

Key Phrases:

- The analysts' personality and reputation and investment ideas [thought leaders in our areas of expertise]
- Price and personality [people they want to work with] and a multi-touch approach with consistency of all involved
- Analysis that is published, high regard for the analyst
- Knows the owners of private companies in the channel

CONCLUSION

When people use the same phrases, and tell the same stories, the brand becomes alive and full of texture. All you need to do is ask the employees and customers what they think and you will know the power of the brand – you'll have all the words needed to communicate what is the truth about the organization.

Defining a Better Way to Operate

Transactional Analysis and Behavioral Alignment System

INTRODUCTION

I'd like to discuss what I think is a major issue facing most of American businesses and government agencies: The fact that we as Americans are becoming more divisive, cynical, angry, and disconnected than at any other time in the last 50 years.

We are now confronted with the fact that major questions are being fought over by groups of people with polarizingly strong core beliefs. These groups have become convinced that their answer to the question is the only right answer; dialogue, listening and compromise have been replaced with blaming, yelling, and "my way or no way."

Greed seems to be rewarded and celebrated with no regard to impact on everyone else. The value of the common worker is now being treated more as capital expense than a valued asset.

When things go wrong, we seem focused on assigning blame, not toward solutions and discussion on how we should fix or improve the situation. I could go on, but I think you get my point.

IMPACT OF SOCIAL MEDIA

A change has taken place in the way we communicate. The social media revolution and the fact the we are now all walking around with a handheld device, which is more of a computer than phone, has created a generational divide as to what a discussion is.

> *Conversation for younger people is a trail of text messaging.*

Twitter has created a substitute for a paragraph of information. Now it's a short group of words.

Everyone with an opinion now has more ways to "go viral." Yelp ratings, Angie's list and Google searches give instant hits on how the business has been rated, directly influencing how new customers perceive the business being evaluated.

The question then becomes: In this current environment, how do you create a culture of employees and customers who are loyal and active evangelists for supporting your business?

ROADBLOCKS FOR AMERICAN BUSINESS AND GOVERNMENT AGENCIES

As we try to define this question, I would like to first define what I think is a major issue facing American business and governmental agencies.

I became interested in the concept of culture and leadership while I was at the University of Washington as a college basketball player: How do you get 12 young men to understand the coach's system and play their role in helping the team be successful?

I received two extra years of university education, earning my MBA while acting as the graduate assistant basketball coach, When it came time to write my thesis, I decided to focus on what then was called "Theory X vs. Theory Y," or democratic vs. autocratic leadership.

I contrasted the coaching styles of two great college coaches: Marv Harshman and Tex Winter, both Hall of Fame coaches. Coach Harshman tailored his system to match the skills and talent of his players, while Coach Winter only allowed the players to work within his system.

I discovered that both styles could be very successful and that the real issue was getting the players to "own" the system and be accountable for playing their role within that system.

I have found the same to be true for regular business and government employees. I am now going to describe my view of a system that develops a culture of employees and customers who are loyal, and who become active evangelists for supporting your business.

I am calling this the Transactional Analysis Behavioral Alignment Operating System. First, I will describe how this system works, and then will recount a few culture change experiences that will bring this system to life.

TRANSACTIONAL ANALYSIS BEHAVIORAL ALIGNMENT OPERATING SYSTEM

This system is grounded in two basic concepts:

First Concept

The discussion of people's attitudes and the impact on how they behave. We have all worked with people who seem to have bad attitudes, and have watched managers try to ignore or deal with these individuals. In most cases the effort is disruptive and many times divisive to the other employees.

I believe that having clearly defined behaviors that are understood and rewarded, will take care of any and all attitude issues.

Second Concept

In any business/governmental operation, every activity is managed through a series of human transactions.

The key is to make sure during each of these transactions that the core behaviors are identified and defined, so that there are clear expectations as to how people should manage their behavior.

This is actually a very simple process; so let me tell you a story that will help you understand this process.

EXPERIENCE

Virginia Mason – Helping to Re-Think a Clinic

I was asked by my personal physician if I would participate in a one-week brainstorm to help totally rework a Virginia Mason Medical Clinic. Because the Kirkland Clinic was moving to a new location, there was an opportunity to radically reorganize the way the clinic worked.

Virginia Mason has a very large investment in looking at their business [a hospital and 12-15 clinics] through the eyes of Toyota University: Lean, efficient and very user-driven.

We started this one-week brainstorm with an end in mind: Greater efficiency for everyone, including the doctors, nurses, specialists, and lastly [why I was there], for the customer. In the end, it was an amazing week.

For five days, 25 people [doctors, nurses, clinic managers, architects – everyone in the business] went through this very formal process to:

- Cut the number of steps a doctor and nurse walk by 50%
- Manage the supply of all the medical things needed to do their work with a just-in-time approach
- Let the patients become a bigger part of the system

So there I was, experiencing a discovery process that used the Toyota Production Management method to re-engineer the entire way a medical clinic operated.

The end of this story is that the Virginia Mason Kirkland Clinic opened in March of 2009, and has accomplished everything that it set out to do with regard to improving efficiency.

As expected, some of the older patients had some trouble with the changes. One of the efforts was to eliminate the clinic waiting rooms – efficiency means no waiting.

As the patient representative, I was not old enough to understand that older patients go to their medical clinics weekly and they like to talk to other weekly visitors at the clinic. Oh well, so much for efficiency.

The basic tool to design the space was a concept they called the "Fish," which really was just a process of engagement – thinking through a transaction and defining all of the steps that the patient needed to take and matching those transaction points with what the clinic employees had to do.

In this diagram, there are two sides – the patient [customer] and the organization. The steps involved for each side are listed to examine efficiencies. For example:

Patients have to park, so the clinic had to think about what getting into the parking lot was like, and how big the stalls should be for their patients. How do older people get out of their cars, then get into clinic?

The next transaction interaction was checking in – what does the patient do and what could be done to ensure when they showed up, the checking in process was efficient?

When the appointment reminder call was made, what could be done to ensure their visit went well – both efficient and an outstanding experience.

Every step in the patient's visit and every system in the clinic's business operation went through a "Fish" process. Notes were kept, priorities were established, and policies, procedures and behaviors were defined.

Learning #1 – You can look at any operational transaction and create a transaction "Fish" approach to understanding what behaviors, policies and procedures must go right every time for the user to have an outstanding experience.

Learning #2 – You can involve your employees and customers

in defining the behaviors of the "Fish" to add real insight and valuable consciousness to how things should work more efficiently, and how to create a dynamic and measurable experience for the user.

Learning #3 – This process transfers ownership to the employees. They become vested in not only how it should work, but also as the behaviors become the work standard, they champion the cultural change in the organization. Management is listening to the employees and customers before they try to change the culture. Attitude follows ownership of the behaviors.

So, when someone starts talking about cultural change, they are talking about changing the very fabric of how things get done, and how this knowledge is transmitted to the next generation. If you want to change a culture, it is more about behaviors than attitudes.

Well-defined behaviors, measured consistently and frequently, are the pathway to cultural change.

Attitudes follow consistent behaviors. Behaviors do not follow better attitudes.

IN SUMMARY

The Transactional Analysis and Behavioral Alignment System

The goal of this system is to align hiring expectations, training, frequent quality assurance reviews, annual reviews, user feedback and an employee reward effort into a consistent, well understood, and totally accepted behavioral standard.

At the beginning of this conversation I suggested that one of the major issues facing both American businesses as well as governmental agencies was the question: In this current environment, how do you create a culture of employees and customers that are loyal and active evangelists for supporting your business?

I believe that there are five steps to answering this question:

1. Clarify your behavior expectations by looking at all of the transactions involved in employee and customer interactions. Then, clearly communicate and train staff toward those behaviors.

2. Be relentless at acknowledging, rewarding and celebrating people who consistently demonstrate those behaviors.

3. Find ways to involve your customers in giving lots of feedback and share it with your employees.

4. Find ways to add surprises for both your employees and customers in their interactions.

5. Constantly listen to the stories that your employees and customers tell about your business. The power of loyal evangelist employees and customers can be measured by the stories they tell.

Transactional Analysis and Behavioral Alignment System Benefits:

• Efficient, effective, and inexpensive

• Lowers turnover and saves significant $$

• Can be implemented without lots of group meetings and expensive speakers

• Will help create a better working culture – and improve attitudes

• Will produce loyal and active evangelist employees and customers, helping businesses to thrive in the new reality of American consumer environment

These Thoughts Come From Unlocking Generational Codes

by Anna Liotta: excerpted from pages 126, 127-131, 155-157

Companies that want to hire and retain top talent need to get up to speed with the goals and preferences of Gen Xers and Millenials while not letting the viewpoints of Baby Boomers stop the technology's progress and the company's future.

The days of loyalty to company are gone, so companies must understand what their employees want, set clear expectations of employees' job duties, and live up to their promises from day one if they do not want to spend extra time, money, and energy on recruiting, only to lose employees.

Following World War II, G.I.s returned from the front and instituted the leadership training and organizational foundation learned in the trenches.

Today, many legacy terms and philosophies such as: chain-of-command leadership, officers of the company, all hands meetings, decisions "above my pay grade," and lockstep compensation plans still influence the thinking and expectations of high-level management.

For most of history, generations have been separated in the workplace due to the hierarchical system inherited from the military leadership and experiences of the G.I/ Veteran generation. Work peers entering the workforce were predominately close in age and generational perspectives.

Today, a leader must adapt his style according to the Generational CODES of the people he is leading. Traditionalists and Boomers are still stunned to be taking orders from someone half their age whom they quietly mutter is still wet behind the ears.

It goes all the way to the top as evidenced in a June 27, 2011 Newsweek interview with retiring Pentagon boss Robert Gates when he said, "Hillary [Clinton] and I call ourselves the Old Folks Caucus... And I must say, it's the first time in my life I've worked for a president who was 20 years younger than I was."

TRADITIONALISTS:

Traditionalists believed in the promises of big institutions and organizations. The golden horizon was that one day you would have the seniority, and then it would be your turn to be the boss, call the shots, lead the troops. In the meantime, you gave your best, and waited with

the expectation that eventually, the best would be returned to you.

For Traditionalists a "healthy" fear of the boss/commanding officer was considered wise. It was understood that moving forward was directly correlated to staying on the boss's good side and making the boss look good.

Traditionalists obeyed the chain of command and "dug in" to their place in the organization's hierarchy. They followed the rules of the day and became "company men," and for the most part, their expectations were met.

Times have changed.

BABY BOOMERS:

Baby Boomers flooded the workforce with high hopes for the world and even higher expectations of changing the way work was done. With their secure childhood during the

> *"Although Boomers may not like to remember it this way, they were considered very difficult to manage..."*

rise of productivity and growth in the High social mood behind them, young Boomers entered the workforce ready to challenge the authority and question

"the man." As young adults of the Consciousness Revolution, Boomers advocated turning the traditional corporate hierarchy upside down.

Although Boomers may not like to remember it this way, they were considered very difficult to manage, and their entry into the workforce was not met with huge upticks in productivity. Why? They were arguing with everyone about everything, and if they weren't happy about how they were being treated, they encouraged their peers to argue as well.

G.I. and Traditionalist bosses saw their questioning and challenging attitudes as rude, entitled, difficult to manage, and oh yes, lacking in strong work ethic. Sound familiar?

Boomers were genuinely passionate about bringing fun and spirit into the workplace, but the reality fell a little short of the big goal. While Boomers read, talked, and shared their ideas and theories of egalitarian leadership and participative management, with 80 million peers/competitors, Baby Boomers quickly began learning the rules of the game and how to work the system. Non-Boomers who work for a Boomer boss will tell you that their boss's career habits, formed from working for command-and-control

Traditionalists and G.I.s, are often still very much in evidence.

GEN XERS:

With the boom of the 1970s ending with the bust of the '80s recession, Gen Xers watched their parents scrape and scrap to climb the corporate ladder while hating their bosses, leaders, and jobs, but still basing their self-worth on the awards and

"Xers saw their parent(s) work twenty-hour days and give up "quality time" with their family to work late and impress the boss."

recognition delivered by those same people and institutions. Xers saw their parent(s) work twenty-hour days and give up "quality time" with their family to work late and impress the boss.

Xers' innocence was stripped away when hard times hit and their parents were cut loose without warning in the prevailing economic recession winds of "down-sizing and right-sizing" for the company's benefit.

Consequently, Xers are suspicious of all "corporate speak." While prior generations believed in the companies that made social contracts with employees, such as, "You work

hard for us and we'll take care of you," Xers know firsthand that the corporate vision, mission, and values are generally only aspirational at best, and more accurately, would be found under the genre of science-fiction or fantasy.

Xers feel like they are in a never-ending search to find a (work) place to call home and leaders whom they can trust and believe. Along with broken promises in the workplace, Xers experienced up close the moral bankruptcy of leaders at every level of private and public institutions.

Observing the first Presidential resignation in US history just as they were beginning to become politically aware fundamentally shaped their belief in the lack of sanctity in public servants.

From Exxon spills to Enron chills, Xers may have hoped for the best, but their core survivor mentality kept telling them to prepare for the worst just when they thought it was "safe to get back in the water." (Duh dunt, Duh Dunt - Imagine scary Jaws music playing in the background, Xers do.)

MILLENIALS:

Millenials respect authority, but they do not fear it. Millenials had formative years filled with fans, friends, coaches, cheerleaders, and BFFs (Best Friend Forever).

With Boomer parents wearing the BFF status as a medal of

accomplishment, Millenials were encouraged to call their parents by their first names from birth and their grandparents by nicknames (Nana, Pop Pop).

> ## *Consequently, Millenials have a very casual relationship with elders and authority figures.*

Parents knew what they should do, but the threat of their children not liking them, or making a public scene was enough to dissuade them from pushing the issue. From the time they were in diapers to texting at the dinner table, Millenials prevailed every time they challenged their Boomer parents. Boomers' commitment to being "liked" by their children meant removing the implementation of penalties or consequences for disobeying the leader/parent.

No longer do we have the unquestioning, follow-the-rules Traditionalists in charge; now authoritarians are on trial. Boomer parents have organized the PTA into a significant political entity to fight collectively and individually on behalf of their Millenials when authoritative figures, such as teachers, attempt to discipline or punish their children.

OLD MODEL/NEW MODEL

- Manager/Coach
- Superior/Peer
- Boss/Partner

Expectations for what defines a work environment have undergone a radical transformation.

A key question that today's top talent is asking when considering a new workplace is, "Will I thrive here?"

> ## *"Traditionalists didn't believe work was supposed to be the place you go to be happy..."*

It's no longer acceptable merely to survive your company, harassing boss, or jerk co-worker. Today's top talent wants your organization's environment to be a place where they will flourish and grow their skills.

Traditionalists didn't believe work was supposed to be the place you go to be happy, find fulfillment, and express your personality or life purpose. A Traditionalist says, "Work is called "WORK" for a reason. Work is a serious place you go to get a real day's work done."

In the 1930s and 1940s, work environment laughter on the job was a disciplinary offense. You could be sacked at the Henry Ford Motor Plant for smiling or

whistling on the job. (Whistle while you work was a Disney-invented fantasy.)

Boomers entered the workforce desiring an egalitarian environment that allowed for a free flow of ideas and opinions, a Utopia.

However, their formative experiences of competing for every opportunity with their Boomer peers quickly transformed each job, bid, and client opportunity into a game full of politics and intrigue to be won at all costs.

Xers entered the workplace with great trepidation, and today, they are viewing the demand that they move into higher levels of management with the same caution.

For Xers, moving up the "ladder" means becoming the enforcer of environmental protocol and policies they don't believe in.

Xers find navigating the political waters and intricate relationship mazes of the Baby Boomers exhausting and unfulfilling. They are creating their own work environments that include: "No Jerk Policies" and "Results-Only Work Environments" (ROWE).

At the other end of the spectrum, the core of a Millenial's definition of work is: "Work is a personally fulfilling experience of creating a solution from wherever I am most productive." For Millenials, work is a state of self-expression. It's not a place where you go to do something; it's what you do from wherever you are. They are looking for fun, friendly, and fast-paced environments that facilitate collaboration and rapid advancement.

While leaders know the cost of talent-turnover is high, they often ignore the hard truth that it's frequently a problem they create. Today's talent expects to see the "promised" company values and culture sold to them in the "romancing" interview stage of the courtship to stand up over time.

Xers and Millenials are clear that they spend the majority of their waking hours in their professional organization's environment. Whether or not they tell you so, top talent joins you on a trial basis all the while withholding judgment on how long they will stay.

The 90-day trial period is now a double-sided decision.

If the answer to their questions of thrive or survive is, "No, I will not thrive here," then they will begin looking, quietly, for a place where they will. Your investment of time, resources, and talent to attract the best and the brightest

is wasted when you quickly lose them because they were sold on an environment the company couldn't or wouldn't provide."

In order to thrive with all three generations working together, everyone has to be ALL-IN accepting some core beliefs:

1. Individual behaviors like listening to understand, not to find a place to speak.

2. Organizational processes that everyone understands and supports.

3. Decision competency – decisions are made at the right time.

4. Everyone is passionate to support the ongoing mission and works hard together to deliver desired outcomes.

Collaborative culture is the only way this will work.

Employee Reward Programs

In all business cultures, people get rewarded. These rewards are in the form of titles, more interesting work projects, invitations to key social functions, deeper working relationships with senior managers, recognition through formal rewards, and, of course, more salary.

When an individual is rewarded, everyone in the organization is put on notice that it is the way to act.

Also, once an individual is rewarded, employees make judgments about the fairness of the reward system. This judgment of fairness goes much deeper than just formal rewards – the entire review process also plays directly into employee judgments about fairness in the organization.

In many companies, reward programs are part of fostering a competitive climate that senior management feels is healthy. The employee with the most sales wins, or the one with the best quarterly production numbers.

Most of these rewards are tied to short-term results and in each case, as the culture develops, other employees form opinions about what is really important

here and how fair the company is.

Rewards go a long way in creating an organizational culture.

Be careful who you reward. They are winners and everyone else is a loser.

The most powerful rewards program, one that will drive an organization forward, is one that enables a passionate workforce committed to success. This requires that you a have a clear and well understood set of expected behaviors that management relentlessly rewards and celebrates.

When employees see that this is not about a winner and a bunch of losers – everyone can be celebrated and recognized – the culture changes to one that has fun winning.

This reward strategy also has a huge side effect: The more people see that employees who excel at the desired behaviors are celebrated, the less of a problem the outliers become. The group starts to place social pressure on either conforming to the behavior standards or finding a new place to work.

Instead of people waiting to see what the manager is going to do with the BAD ATTITUDE EMPLOYEE, the team takes on the responsibility for the behavior of the team.

As I mentioned before, putting a customer feedback tool into the Tully's operation more than proved that this "reward clear behaviors" model works wonders.

We identified six basic questions that a customer could rate as to how the store staff performed these clearly defined behavior expectations.

We then posted their weekly scores on those six questions next to the employee work schedule. If one of the behaviors had a low score, the team made sure that everyone was ALL-IN to change the score in the future by adjusting behaviors.

All management had to do was celebrate and reward the group for high customer scores. There was a business reward for the manager, [the overall store rating was a score between 1 and 5, with 5 being great and 1 being poor] and there was a 100% correlation to business performance. If the average of all six questions was 4.5-5.0, the store was running over 8% increases, if the average score was 4.0-4.5, the store was running even sales, and if the average score was below 4.0, then that store had a negative sale performance.

The store team managed the effort of getting great scores – what you reward is what you get.

HOW TO ASSESS

Through a series of one-on-one interviews with employees in different levels of the organization, you can determine a great deal about what is highly rewarded in the organizational culture.

1. Does the company have a formal reward program? Describe it.

2. Does everyone in the company have an equal opportunity to be rewarded?

3. Do the same people always seem to be rewarded?

4. Does the company have any rewards for teams of people?

5. Do you have a clear understanding of the behaviors that are expected?

6. Are there team awards?

7. How are rewards given out?

8. Do you care if you receive a reward?

9. Outside of the formal reward program, describe other ways you have seen people rewarded.

OUTCOMES

An organization's reward program will help determine what type of culture the organization has.

The key to rewards are:

• Do they build a sense of common focus, or create individual competitions between coworkers?

• Do they help build a sense of fairness, or do favorite people seem to always win?

A sustainable high-performance culture will have people wanting to be rewarded for outstanding performance.

How to Focus and Edit Your Workload

Most bureaucracies with more than two levels of management consistently suffer from having too much to do, and too many people wanting to do too many things.

I once had a boss who had three simple rules for his subordinates framed on his wall:

Rule #1 – Make your boss happy.

Rule #2 – Read rule #1 again.

Rule #3 – Do what you want to do.

These three rules served as a constant reminder that no matter what an employee feels is important, what the boss wants is always more important.

Though I feel that in most organizations the manager-employee relationship works this way, the critical factor is the amount of control the boss wants or needs to have. The more control, the less of Rule #3 the employee gets to do.

"I believe that the most motivated organizations are the ones in which the bosses get what they want..."

If you remember, one of the major premises of my management philosophy is that:

People will do what they think they ought to do, how they think they should do it.

When a major conflict arises between a boss and subordinate, it ends up determining the level of freedom and participation people feel is allowable in the work environment.

I believe that the most motivated organizations are the ones in which the bosses get what they want because the employees perceive it as something they want to do. Their goal becomes not merely to make the boss happy, but to add their personal intensity and creative enhancements to the projects and tasks at hand.

The gap between just getting the priorities of the boss accomplished and a more participatory system of involved employees, calls for a process of focusing and editing. A creative environment can spawn many ideas and concepts, but if there isn't a quality focus and edit process in place, then a lot of hard working, energized people will force the manager to become more autocratic, thus destroying all efforts to involve them.

The challenge and fine line of balance is having a process that facilitates the subordinates' involvement, while allowing the boss to be comfortable with a clear focus and edit approach that directs their energy.

The most important element of developing a focused and edited list of priorities is a strong base concept of what your business is and the key strategies you are counting on to deliver success. There is an old adage that a poor plan, well executed, will always beat a great plan that no one follows.

Great companies have global plans that integrate all areas of the business with a clear idea of how each area enhances the whole. No matter what part of the organization you are in charge of, if you can't articulate your area's strategies, and define how the completion of your tasks fits into the company's overall strategy, you have a problem.

Often, the best way to avoid a lack of focus in your area is to use calendars showing six month's worth of tasks at a

time. When are the planning periods? When do the weekly reports become due, and what amount of time does it take to accomplish either the compiling of the reports or reacting to them? When do all the meetings take place and how do the meetings affect planning and reacting?

You should look at your job description to determine what tasks must be accomplished to meet the requirements of your job.

- When do you focus on personnel issues?
- When are the reviews done?
- Have you left enough time or do you expect that they will be done right and with thought within your normal schedule?

The calendar helps you understand what constitutes priorities of your people, and occupies their thoughts.

In order to focus and edit you must have a big picture, and you must know what is needed to complete it.

Managers cannot take charge of their area and be proactive in managing their portion of the business without understanding:

- The tasks to be accomplished

- The timing required
- The effect on the overall company strategy

The alternative to this is that each day you and your people walk into the office and wait for the phone to ring. It is your boss and whatever is asked for that becomes the immediate priority of the day. Your constant focus is to react, react, react.

The whole organization is limited to the ability of one person – your boss. Whatever is on his or her mind at that moment is the company's priority. This answers Rules #1 and #2. Your boss is happy, and in making him or her happy, you secure your job.

But what happens when the boss is fired, which is inevitable in the long run?

Hiring the Right People

In the current technological world, all the social changes that are happening in how we do things, along with the convergence of three different generations in the workplace who view the world from different generational perspectives, can provoke many questions for management. One question in particular can be a game changer:

HOW DO YOU HIRE THE RIGHT PEOPLE?

What a great question. I have already suggested that the first thing you need to have in your mind is what kind of culture you are building.

If most of the work that needs to be accomplished is individually managed and there is very little group collaboration required – then you will be looking for someone with a totally different personality and skill set than is needed to work in a highly collaborative and integrated culture. ***The first thing is to know your culture.***

Once you are aware of the culture, you can then move on to the basic question of what type of skills are required.

The second thing you need to define is whether the skills are trainable, or do you need a level of skill experience. The point to this is, if the skills are trainable you can put more focus on the personality, talents, curiosity, empathy, and fun human traits – knowing that training the skills will be easy if you hire the right attitudes.

So how do you hire a person that has personility, talents, curiosity, empathy, and fun as their core traits?

The way to understand the person you are hiring is to know the right questions to ask. I'm assuming that the hiring process has the requirement to submit a resume, and that once you form an opinion, you will call references [I will discuss this later in this section]. So what are the right questions? Here are my favorites:

1. I have looked at your resume and it has some very strong experiences. What would you like me to know about what your resume says about you?

2. What are the best two things you have learned in the last two years?

3. When your supervisor has not been clear about defining your role in the organization, what do you do?

4. Describe an experience you have had working in a team environment and tell me what you learned from that experience.

5. Describe a situation where you were managing a project, and what you learned from that experience.

6. You are sitting in a team meeting discussing a problem; you know what the solution should be, but a different solution seems to be winning. What do you do?

7. When you disagree with a coworker, what do you do?

8. What will your references say about you when I ask? Tell me what it is like to work with you.

9. Any questions for me about this opportunity?

OBTAINING REFERENCES: HOW TO APPROACH

References are usually individuals who will say good things about the person you are checking on – in most cases, they will just provide confirmation of the personal opinion you have developed during the hiring process.

I would suggest that you might put a small speed bump in the final hiring element. Ask for at least three references:

1. A person who they have worked for.

2. A person who they have worked with.

3. A person who worked for them.

This approach allows for 360-degree feedback on the individual – and will serve as a confirmation that people throughout the work environment see the same person at work.

Impact of a Social Environment on a Collaborative Working Culture

"There is something deeply important about an experience of being in the presence of someone without being impinged upon by their demands, and without them needing to make a demand on you. And this creates a space where someone can feel sufficiently safe as though there is a shield, or someone guarding you against dangers such that you can be forget your self and be open to trust of and connection to others."

- *The Paris Review* with Adam Phillip

IT ALL STARTS WITH A CONVERSATION

CONVERSATION: A form of interactive spontaneous communication between two or more people who are following the rules of etiquette. It's a polite give and take of subject thought by talking with each other for company.

- How well do you engage individuals and small groups

in conversation that allows for equal exchange of information?

- How comfortable are you with engaging, considering the time pressures of your workday?

In all of the management positions I have had, getting to know people as associates or human beings was many times more important than only knowing them as employees.

> *Knowing people's values and understanding how they are handling their entire life, is the only way that a collaborative working environment can be accomplished.*

When I started my own business, Treats, which was a neighborhood restaurant and dessert house, we treated the employees as a family. If we got busy when the employees were in the building as customers, they would pop up, bus tables, deliver food, and clean up – without being asked.

They all shared the vision and felt accountable to making Treats successful.

When I was given the job as director of training for The Bon Marché, I was also given the responsibility to organize and produce the employee reward effort.

Our big focus was six regional Achiever Banquets. These events were all at very nice resort facilities where the top sale associates would come in for what amounted to a very fun party.

All management would be there and each store's top sale producers would enjoy a great dinner, open bar and after-dinner dancing, where everyone was just having fun.

The entire organization looked forward every spring to what I call the Achiever Road Show. As I reflect back on these banquets, what I remember most is that this was the one time a year where management and key sales associates were just a bunch of people having a lot of fun. The conversations were not about work, they were about just getting to know each other.

Very often the groups that attended these events were the same year after year. In some ways we all just became friends, having a great time at a very fun party.

When management traveled to these stores for business reviews, the way people interacted changed. People played less attention to their titles and spent more time just discussing business objectives

with people they knew. Working together was fun, not stressful.

When I was given the opportunity to take over the in-house advertising agency, the unit was very polarized.

Many of the staff had been in the operation for a long time, and the work groups were very separated – both in their social interactions as well as how they did their work.

The previous senior leadership was very hands off and did not spend any time in the agency. In those days the senior leadership was on the 7th floor and the agency was on the 3rd floor.

When I was given the assignment, it happened congruently with the retirement of the operating vice president. Being curious, I decided to do both the senior vice president job and the operation vice president function. I had two offices: One on the 7th floor and the other on the 3rd floor, right in the middle of the aagency operation.

I lasted in the senior VP position for almost 11 years. One of the most important elements of being able to turn this dysfunctional high-production agency into a high-performing and technology-leading collaborative organization was the hiring of my administrative assistant, Colleen Bol.

With Colleen, we not only doubled productivity, but Colleen added the title of DIRECTOR OF FUN to her job description.

Throughout the 18 years of working together, as we moved into helping Seattle Community Colleges define their vision for the upcoming millennium, to spending six years as the head of alumni relations for the University of Washington, and finally as the CEO of Tully's Coffee, Colleen was not only a terrific assistant, helping organize my heavy meeting and event schedule, but more importantly, she paid attention to the social aspect of our cultures.

I have often told Colleen, and anyone else who would listen, she made me look better than I was.

The lessons learned:

- People who work together and play together, stay together.

- People who work together and play together, manage change together.

- People who work together and play together, handle crises together.

- People who work together and play together, produce more work together.

- People who work together and play together, stay friends together.

A truly collaborative working environment must be built on a consistent execution of many things, but all of the management behaviors that support collaborative cultures are greatly improved when people know their fellow employees as real human beings.

This "real people" interaction increases trust, creates greater empathy, makes change easier, and supports passion and positive self-esteem, both for the individual and the team.

It all starts with a conversation...

Job Descriptions: A Forgotten Asset

In the middle of one of my many management learning experiences, I was struck with how difficult it was to get every employee focused on a single picture of success, and to see how each of their own jobs fit into it.

Things I have learned:

- You cannot hire a new employee or change your organizational chart without first rewriting the job descriptions

- It is impossible to review an employee without having a clear job description

- Job descriptions and an organizational chart are the basis of any organization

- All personnel issues start, and sometimes finish, with the quality of job descriptions

- Public institutions do a better job of using job descriptions to hire people and define a potential new employee's responsibilities than private institutions

I truly believe that private business often fails to use the discipline of effective job descriptions to define employee responsibilities and their roles in the organization as a whole.

When I was first given the responsibility of running the Marketing and Sales Promotion division at The Bon Marché, I felt I needed to learn what people did, so I asked the personnel department to give me the job descriptions for my division.

I found that there were very few complete ones and that the previous senior manager preferred to have not only as few as possible, but to also make them very general.

The belief was that the less people knew about what others were doing, the better. I spent a better part of two months rewriting all the job descriptions myself.

This exercise taught me a great deal:

- The relationships of tasks between different employee groups
- The expectations I had for the area managers
- How the jobs of leads differ from those of standard employees

Seeing who could make what decisions and who was responsible for what proved to be not only a quick way to learn my new area, but also created many questions that in turn, generated a whole list of structures and employee relationships that I wanted to challenge. On the whole, I found it to be a great experience.

As I continued to restructure and redefine the organization to meet the many challenges of the day-to-day operation, I always focused first on the job descriptions and the organizational chart, knowing they had to be rewritten prior to any structural move.

In each case, the reward for adherence to this goal was employees having a better understanding of the issues and changes of the new structure.

The true test of this use of job descriptions came when we decided to redo our entire production process, from traditional manual methods to a massive electronic publishing system. In this transition the approach was proven, and even enhanced. We began with choosing what form of electronic publishing to use. There were two options.

1. The first was an IBM system that had been designed to match the existing work flow, and duplicated many of the specific job functions of the traditional manual production system. It made the existing environment electronic, with a high output capacity.

2. The second option was an Apple Macintosh system that was very design-oriented. It established a work flow, production output, and job descriptions that were entirely different from the traditional manual production process.

We searched the United States for an organization using something like what we were considering, but could not find anybody with as big a system as we required.

It was obvious from our studies that we needed the creative environment offered by the Macintosh, but we were worried that we might have output problems.

We finally decided to risk the output problems because we felt the future would more easily correct Macintosh's output than IBM's creative gaps.

Once the decision was made, my senior team set about the task of rewriting the job descriptions and organizational charts of our new organization. *What a learning experience!*

First, we were not sure what the exact job descriptions, job

"The descriptions formed the rationale for why some employees were not retained..."

functions, and job tasks would be. We were not sure how much of a workload individuals would be able to handle. The personalities of the people who traditionally dealt with our clients generally didn't match those of people who worked on the computers.

But in spite of these obstacles, we created job descriptions, reorganized our organizational charts, planned how to find new employees, decided on our severance packages and retraining programs, established our transition plan, and took off.

The job descriptions first allowed us to reposition employees into jobs their existing skills qualified them for and showed us how much training they would require to stay in the new job environment.

The descriptions formed the rationale for why some employees were not retained, and established

job requirements for new employees.

From the personnel side, I would say the transition was smooth. New employees were hired, some employees preferred to leave, some were asked to leave, and some were retrained.

After 100 days of trying to force the production from the old system to the new, we hit a major wall. The new system was running at full capacity.

Both new and old employees were working very hard, but no one knew for certain what the new work flow was, who made which decisions, or who was responsible for what function.

Large sums of money were being spent to get the work done outside, and the overall stress level was creating attitudes of distrust, disrespect, blaming, and potential explosion among employees.

I received an anonymous letter from an employee stating that, in their opinion, we were on the verge of a total breakdown in all parts of the organization.

Defining a better way to operate.

I must admit this was a very difficult time, and as the senior manager, I had to take responsibility. I knew that even though we worked hard at putting a good plan for transition together, it had succeeded only in giving the employees new jobs and tasks – and that was it.

At that moment I clearly understood crisis management, issue management and standards and procedures management. We had created standards and procedures, but unknown issues had caused a crisis.

This is reinforced by what I call the Principle of the Unintended Consequence, which states:

No matter what the plan or intent, the unintended will always overpower the intended.

After we moved into crisis management, we clearly narrowed our focus, established priorities, defined important issues, and started to manage our way out of the production crisis. But getting work out the door was not going to fix the organization. It was not going to reestablish people's respect and trust in each other. More needed to be done.

Now the use of job descriptions went to a new level. In the past I had always been the one to write the job descriptions and use them to define people's roles in my organization.

"We then went around the room and each person read their job description out loud."

I realized that nobody knew what the new organization was going to look like. I needed a new approach – one that would take the strength and discipline of the job descriptions and let the employees empower themselves for a new culture, a new work flow, and a new environment.

I started where I had always started, with me looking at the job descriptions. But this time I handed them out to everybody in the organization. I scheduled meetings with each work group in which we discussed their job descriptions, their functions, responsibilities and tasks.

Then I asked, "What issues are in the way of getting these tasks done?" Each meeting started the same way, with me acknowledging that the activities of the last few weeks had created a need to redefine our roles and functions in the organization.

We then went around the room and each person read their job

136 • The Loyalty Solutions Group

description out loud. People were asked if they agreed with what was being read and whether any of the statements required clarification.

Finally, we discussed what issues were getting in the way of their ability to do the job.

If job functions between different work groups were not clearly defined, a second meeting was scheduled with the two groups to discuss the issues and make decisions on how to proceed.

Within 30 days of this exercise, the new organization was communicating and operating at a higher level than the best of the traditional organizations.

> *People were trusting each other and helping each other solve problems.*

Job descriptions are basic to any organization. Using this tool as a means of employee empowerment can significantly enhance the overall production level and job satisfaction level of every employee.

I never let a year go by without meeting with every employee group to discuss their jobs and what issues are in the way of their performance.

The Use of Reviews

As long as I have been in the business world, I have participated in the review process. *No matter how many times I have been given a review, and no matter how positive the review has been, there have always been one or two comments I have taken as highly negative.*

In fact, in some managers' minds, the best way to use reviews is to put people down and create a great deal of insecurity. Regardless of how little or great the negatives are, they always lead to a sense of insecurity in the employee's behavior.

The comments are generally remembered for the entire year. In moments of stress, these comments become the mental battleground for the employee's level of passive resistance.

There are many methods of using reviews, but I have found a couple of extremely useful techniques to make sure an employee is never surprised by a manager's evaluation.

Differences in perception of a person's performance should be identified for what they really are: Two people observing one's behavior from different points of view. I firmly believe that most review problems come from differences in values – how you spend your time, how you spend

your money, and how you treat other people.

Usually, a review form has been designed by a personnel department as a general document with the assumption that all employees can be rated evenly and with the same form.

The problem with this is that all the jobs in the company have specific tasks and requirements that make a general form inappropriate. This can create problems.

Most review forms have a closing section that asks:

1. What are the person's strengths?

2. What are the person's weaknesses?

3. What is the plan to help improve the employee's performance?

It is also true that most review periods take place after the closing of the business year, when all the numbers are in.

I began to develop a very successful tool, that is used to to pre-review all employees 3-4 months prior to the formal company review period. This allows them to begin working on

improving their performances, and makes the formal review process a no-surprise event.

I take the three questions above and have each manager fill in their answers 3-4 months before the formal period. This helps the managers identify concerns about their employees before they actually use the review, so they can take disciplinary action if there are problems, and identify positive behaviors that need to be rewarded during the formal period.

Adding the pre-review ensures that the manager and I discuss each employee at least twice a year – not just at review time – and have a chance to find solutions to any problems. This process also eliminates any surprises about employee performance during the formal review.

The pre-review does not have to go in the employee's permanent record, so there is less hesitancy to spell out the entire truth.

Finally, it establishes plans for improvement at the time when most employees are receptive to positive behavioral changes. Most employees know when salary review time is, and behaviors and attitudes always improve 2-3 months before then.

Reviews always boil down to three basic types of communication with the employee.

FIRST IS THE EASIEST:

The employee sees their behavior and performance exactly as you do. You agree on

"You and they see the world totally differently. Where you say they need to improve, they think they are great."

their strengths and weaknesses, and you both agree on a plan to help improve areas that need to be, or can be, improved. These reviews go smoothly and the employees usually get promoted.

SECOND MOST COMMON COMMUNICATION:

The employee is totally at odds with your appraisal of his or her behaviors. The two of you see the world totally differently. Where you say improvement is needed, the employee thinks their performance is great.

This type of review is also very easy. The issues are clearly defined and ultimately the employee is put on notice, removed from the company, or finds a convenient reason to get a new job.

Usually this type of employee creates a lot of bad morale, and until their departure, bad-mouths both the company and the manager at any opportunity. He or she should be helped

out of the company as quickly as possible, though it is also important over the long term to allow this person maximum dignity. The employee may eventually see the light and remember being treated in a compassionate way.

THE LAST FORM OF EMPLOYEE REVIEW COMMUNICATION:

The employee does some things very well or satisfactorily, but has other behaviors that are not appropriate. This makes the review more difficult.

These employees do well enough to stay employed, but create a great deal of mental anguish for a manager because they are constantly being just disruptive enough to cause a problem.

They are very hard to review, because generally they don't believe there is a problem. I suggest that 70-80% of a manager's employee problems happen when dealing with this type of situation.

A technique that I have found very effective in dealing with all three of these situations is comparing a self-review to the formal review.

The technique is very simple. You first devise a simple 3-4 section review that has a 1-5 rating scale.

For instance, if customer service is one section it might only have three statements:

1. Approaches customers in a positive and appropriate manner.
2. Helps customers in handling problems.
3. Customers feel positive after their interaction.

Each of these statements would be rated 1-5, or on a good-to-bad scale.

As a manager, you have to create the questions that best define the behaviors and activities that make for an effective employee.

You fill in your ratings for each employee, and have each rate themselves. Then, you sit down with each employee and compare their scores with yours.

The three types of review communication will become obvious. Most employees will have the same scores as yours – they will be the ones you most enjoy working with.

There will also be a few who rate themselves much lower than you rate them. These employees are in need of greater self-esteem. They are usually some of your best, but are afraid to rate themselves highly. This technique can really help improve their self-image, and

bring them to their full potential.

A small group will give themselves all high marks vs. your low marks. *These are the employees you should help find a new job.*

Finally, there are those employees who match your ratings in some areas, but see their behavior much differently in others. This is where this tool is most valuable. It allows you to say that while you agree with their opinion that their behavior is positive in some areas, there are other areas that the two of you view very differently. You then ask them what should be done about it.

This helps employees see more clearly the differences in perception of their performance, while leaving them with the most dignity. The normal one-way review in this situation tends to focus only on the differences, and does not generate enough conversation about the positive. I believe this process gives you the best and quickest review communication with your employees.

Both of the techniques – the pre-review and the comparison review – are done outside the normal formal review process.

Both should be done prior to the end of the business year. If you are taking over a new territory, these processes are even more useful, in terms of

enhancing communication and building understanding with your employees.

Again, the objective is to make sure that employees are never surprised at your perception of their performance.

"...the objective is to make sure that employees are never surprised at your perception of their performance."

If done positively, the review process is a motivating experience. People walk away with a clear picture of how to achieve success and a comfortable in understanding how they are performing.

They never feel there was a surprise or hidden agenda. If they feel either of these, it leads to passive resistance, potential morale problems, and a fear of the review process.

It is said that the review process is the manager's most powerful tool in motivating their subordinates. It is imperative that reviews help strengthen your organization, not undermine it.

Cross-Training: A Way to Common Values

I have put a great deal of emphasis on a manager's ability to identify his or her values and to make judgments about other people's values as part of the equation of successful organizations.

If you have a value problem – which really means that people have different priorities with regard to how they spend their time, how they spend money or how they treat other people – how do you handle the situation?

My experience is that you can help homogenize a group of people's values with a massive dose of cross-training.

In athletics, people have found that if you specialize in only one type of exercise, the muscles required for that exercise get stronger at the expense of other muscles.

Great athletes now spend a good deal of time cross-training so that all muscle groups grow together. In that way, the body as a whole gets stronger and more flexible and is better able

to withstand injury.

I believe that a group's value system is very similar. If one or two individuals are the only ones who make value decisions about time, money, or personal issues, then the group – like an athlete's body – becomes very strong and distinct, but not flexible, and is prone to more injury and conflicts.

These injuries and conflicts create an increased opportunity for passive resistance to grow. In the end, the group becomes less productive and unable to grow beyond the one or two people who own the high ground on the value system.

> *Cross-training is really a very simple discipline of enhancing the empathy and respect of people toward another worker's point of view.*

The basic premise is that people who understand the pressures, time constraints, costs, and personality styles of others in a work group will have a significantly higher level of empathy for each other. Eventually, they develop a more common value system about spending time, spending money, and how to treat other people.

A word about empathy: I have

grown to believe it is the highest human value, outside of love. To have empathy with another human being, one must be able to respect, trust, understand, and intuitively visualize their situation.

Empathy is basic to the ability of letting another person have a place of dignity in tough situations. It is fundamental to creating win-win situations. It is the foundation of long-term, thriving relationships essential for successful organizations.

The concept of cross-training is really quite easy to understand so I don't feel I need to extend the discussion beyond providing some ideas that have worked for me in the past:

THE LUNCH PRESENTATION

In an organization with many technical components, having a once-a-month lunch where each small group presents what they do to the larger group seems to work very well. We used a potluck format and it had major implications for the group dynamics and overall understanding. This technique also serves to involve the entire work group.

The lowest salaried people to the highest paid, gain a greater understanding of other workers' roles and issues.

MANAGEMENT MEETINGS

Since most management meetings focus on group issues, one idea is to put "managers training" on the agenda each week. Each manager gets a few minutes to explain parts of their organization to the other managers.

GROUP TRAINING SESSIONS

Many bottom-line managers question the value of organized training sessions; these cost time and money and show no immediate return on investment.

Yet outside training is the best way to bring a longer term focus and supportive work environment to any organization.

In most cases the adage that you can lead a horse to water but you can't make him drink, holds true for any training that you institute. But if it is part of your overall business formula, then you never know when you might have a thirsty horse.

A consistent training program gives employees tangible proof that the manager cares about their personal growth. They are also likely to seek help and work through a problem much faster. In addition, these sessions have profound effects on the group's overall communication and development of common values.

EXPLAINING WHY

I believe that when managers make decisions they should spend the time to explain their reasoning to their key subordinates. This is not a justification, but more of a way to let the subordinate start to understand the value system of the boss.

These conversations help dispel mistrust and questions and help force the boss to clarify his or her own decision-making process.

It has become obvious to me that the current pace of American business has put pressure on a manager's ability to incorporate these longer term concepts into one daily management process. Though one could always say "we don't have time," one could also say "we can't afford not to."

If you have a cross-training program in place and value these concepts, I am positive that your organization:

"To have empathy with another human being, one must be able to respect, trust, understand, and intuitively visualize their situation."

1. Communicates better.

2. Handles problems better.

3. Has less passive resistance than work groups that don't believe in the value of cross-training.

Finding Creative Solutions

For any business person in today's environment, the ability to remain on top lies in finding creative solutions to old problems and issues. Most of this guide is about creating a culture that utilizes people's ability to overcome problems. I have discussed, in some depth, issues management and people's values as they relate to the

remains positive. But I contend that basic business survival will be at stake if the company has not empowered its people to be part of the solution process.

There are techniques that can help a manager in any organization tap the knowledge of workers without taking much time or energy.

I am offering these ideas with the assumption that the overall culture is not supportive and that employees have not had much experience with the kind

> *"These solutions require a great deal of employee commitment requiring small attitudinal or behavioral changes on a daily basis."*

creative process. While a few people are looking for significant technological breakthroughs, most of us are trying to find solutions to issues and problems that will affect our business less than 1%.

These solutions require a great deal of employee commitment with small attitudinal or behavioral changes on a daily basis. The only two ways this type of change takes place is through the use of fear or through an engaged workforce that shares a commitment to making a difference.

Fear works for the short term and even over the long term, if the general market situation

of behavior described here. My premise is that if these ideas work in unsupportive cultures, they should work even better in a more positive and group-involved atmosphere.

Generally, the manager realizes there is a problem facing the work group, and the old solutions are not working. The manager does not have the time to recreate the culture and he or she may not have the skills. In most cases the manager will not even want to change the culture; the only objective is to find a new solution.

In most cases of this nature the first thing is to understand that:

> ## The group must go outside the usual range of solutions or choose to find a new way of looking at the problem.

Both of these concepts rest on the idea that we look at problems in light of the history and experiences we bring to the moment, and respond through our personality, with its inherent strengths and weaknesses.

Finding a creative solution to a problem is really nothing more than looking at it through a different set of backgrounds, histories, and personalities. This means that you really have several options, though they are somewhat limited by the amount of money you can spend.

TRAVEL

First, get out and travel – go see how other people do things. A manager in the middle of a serious set of decisions and problems usually becomes myopic and very narrowly focused.

You went into the swamp with the objective to drain it, but you found some alligators. It does not seem important that the alligators are not the same today as yesterday. It's the idea that all alligators are the same and that you still need to drain the swamp.

Leaving the swamp and seeing how other people deal with their swamp and their alligators may provide the creative solution you need. You don't always want to look for swamps that are the same as yours.

When the banks realized they needed a better answer to their customer service problem, they went to retail and the restaurant and hospitality industries looking for their solutions.

As a manager you should always look for ways to send your

> ## "The key element is that you are willing to look outside of your own swamp."

people on experiences that will let them see other organizations and groups who will give them input about their situation while there are still choices to be made.

OUTSIDE INFLUENCE

A second technique is to hire a trained facilitator to come into the environment and create a breakthrough discussion. This usually takes a couple of days to accomplish, but has a major impact on the business environment. It is a clear signal to everybody that something is

different and a different method is being used.

It is highly probable that the immediate issue will receive a fresh look, a different perspective, and that the group going through the experience will be able to vent some frustrations as well as offer ideas and solutions that management has not asked for before.

But if nothing changes after the experience, passive resistance to issues and resistance to participate will increase.

In many ways the choice of an outside facilitator should be made based on whether high turnover is an obstacle to maintaining a meaningful work environment.

The ultimate indicator of employee passive resistance is usually high turnover, either in people who are let go or people who are looking for new jobs.

When the job market is soft, you can have a passive resistant workforce that just hangs around. In any of these cases a one-time visit from a quality outside facilitator can work wonders to help find a new point of view – that includes a lot of employee history – to help solve the problem.

In an environment like the one I have been describing, bringing in an outside facilitator on a consistent basis over several years will not only help solve critical problems, but send a signal to your people that you are interested in their personal growth.

As a result, the level of passive resistance will be significantly diminished. There will be less need for major creative breakthrough, because issue management will be part of the culture.

MEETINGS

A third way to find solutions is to simply call a meeting with your people. Create an atmosphere different enough from your other meetings to let them know it's for a very specific purpose, and use a different technique than you normally use.

Most managers hold meetings in a manner that reflects their work personality. If they are extroverted they gather everybody together to discuss or brainstorm how things should change. If they are introverted they ask everybody to write a quick note and give them some ideas as to how to solve the problem. If the manager is very structured, people talk in turn, and if the manager is spontaneous, the conversation jumps from one idea to another.

The point is, there is no one way to get a breakthrough. However, I will offer a process that balances all the skills and styles, and at least gives you an opportunity to construct an environment that encourages a creative solution.

The premise driving this process is that you must create an atmosphere that is different

the manager assign seats to ensure that people are not sitting with their work friends. The room should have a flip chart, felt pens, and masking tape.

3. The issue or problem should be written on the flip chart so people see it as they enter the room. The first discussion should be to identify and

"...you must create an atmosphere that is different than business-as-usual, and that allows all types of people to participate in the solution."

than business-as-usual, and that allows all types of people to participate in the solution. It also requires the manager to learn one new technique to involve his or her people.

The steps are:

1. Call a meeting with a formal request for attendance and a clear statement of why it is being called: To discuss and find solutions to a very specific problem.

2. Limit the size of the meeting to 15-20 people, and have the room set up in a U-shaped configuration. Most managers have been to a seminar or training meeting in which the organization of the room was designed to promote conversation and discussion. I also suggest that

define the problem so that everybody is clear that it exists and that they are using the same definition.

4. The next step is risky for the manager. I suggest that you buy a book on "mind mapping" and take your people through a mind map of the problem.

The basic premise of mind mapping is that any problem has parts and pieces, and it must first be organized into compatible groups of issues. Problems are solved in small increments, not big pieces.

To define and group the issues allows the problem to be broken down into basic parts, and therefore, more easily solved.

I will not try to explain mind mapping other than to say

it is not a difficult concept, and in this kind of meeting, it is more helpful to the extroverts in the work group. Going around the room, each person adds their thoughts, while the manager uses the mind mapping technique to categorize the comments into common areas.

If an employee does not have anything to say, he or she can pass and wait until the next time around. The idea is to fill a flip chart with issues surrounding the central problem, classifying them into general areas that can be attacked together. This process also shows how different types of issues are related to each other.

5. If there is time after the points of the problem are identified and arranged, break your workgroup into smaller groups with the objective of coming up with solutions to a set of issues.

6. The final step is to have each small group report to the large group their recommendations for solving the issues, including both How and When they would be carried out. This can take from one-and-a-half days to a week or two, depending on the nature of the problem and how the issues come together.

The obvious advantages of this process are that it involves people, clarifies the problem and its key points, and elicits the group's best ideas for a solution. It also has a positive effect on those who participate.

The overall goal of finding a creative solution to management problems is understandable and possible, but I am reminded that only a thirsty horse will drink when led to the water.

If these techniques are part of the overall culture, then the group will be solving issues and problems as part of its everyday work habits. They will always be drinking the water.

If the culture is not in place, then the horse may need to become thirsty in order to find the best creative solution.

Dealing With Poor Performance Employees

No matter how much experience you have had as a manager, the most difficult part of the job is dealing with an employee's poor performance. In fact, one of the most important ways that all organizations can improve their performance is to focus on improving the performance of the bottom 10% of employees.

"...other employees will pay close attention to how you deal with these poorest performing individuals..."

I have a belief that the bottom 10% determine the performance level of 50-60% of the employees that you manage.

People are not naïve – they know who is not engaged and who needs to improve or leave. In fact, in most organizations, people will judge their own performance by making sure that they perform just above the individuals at the bottom.

It is actually worse than that; other employees will pay close attention to how you deal with these poorest performing individuals. The way that you handle this group will have a significant impact on the culture of your organization going forward.

There are many reasons that some employees are not performing at the level you expect. There are outside issues such as:

- Health issues
- Family issues
- Addiction issues

There are also organizational issues, such as:

- Poor training
- Lack of consistent management
- Lack of coaching
- A history of poor reviews that never addressed the problem

All in all, the effort to deal with poor performance, or to not deal with it, is a critical element of building a high-performance work environment.

When dealing with the reasons for poor performance, lots of bad things can happen.

These issues can easily be disruptive to a culture, they can foster divisive relationships inside the culture, and in the end leave you feeling like you are in the middle of a TV soap opera.

The most difficult scenario involves dealing with employees that have low self-esteem and

have learned to use the victim mentality. Most of the time, this creates a passive-aggressive personality that can consume lots of valuable time and energy.

In dealing with the issue of improving a person's poor performance, always be sure you are giving that person their dignity throughout the process.

The worst outcome you can have is finding a way to remove the individual from the organization, but having all of the other employees watch someone lose their dignity.

"You never want the people in your organization to judge your behavior as demeaning and unfair."

Dignity is about someone's self-esteem and your fairness.

You never want the people in your organization to judge your behavior as demeaning and unfair.

In the longer run, their perception of you as a manager will be greatly impacted by your behaviors in handling these situations.

There is a big difference between for-profit, nonprofit, and government agencies in how you deal with poor performing employees.

Nonprofit and government agencies have the most difficult cultural climates, and union contracts can make things even more complicated.

I experienced an example of this when I was the executive director of the University of Washington Alumni Association. This is a State of Washington job. Within the union contract, more highly tenured workers can bump those lower in tenure working a similar classified job if for some reason the higher-tenured worker's position is eliminated.

This creates a unique set of challenges. At a public institution, one of the most important jobs is that of the receptionist.

Alumni associations serve as one of the top first calls alumni will make, to ask just about anything they want to know about the university. The only unit that takes more calls is athletics.

I got a call from one of the campus units: They were closing down their reception position to merge with another unit, it was a union-approved activity, and the union employee had seniority over the receptionist we were currently employing.

Translation:

Our young but very good receptionist, who was receiving unsolicited positive comments, was going to be laid-off and this more senior state employee would be taking her place.

I found out later Why this happened.

Backstory:

This person was a big problem and the other unit did not want to deal with the issue. The only way they could get rid of the individual was to remove the job and give the issue they were unwilling to deal with to some other unit.

Outcome:

You can guess what happened: We started getting complaints immediately. The staff became upset because the original receptionist had made their jobs easier. Now, everything was a problem to solve.

The person was less than one year from retirement, had bad hygiene problems, was very

"...while we were focused on some things that had improved, now we were creating what I could almost not believe: A Hostile Work Environment."

rude to our callers and staff, and had a habit of arriving late and leaving early on a regular basis,

which meant others had to cover the reception desk.

What followed illustrates the complexity of the issue. I called the HR representative to discuss the problem, and in the discussion I asked why we simply couldn't offer a six-month severance and health benefits to take the individual to retirement age. Everybody would be happy.

Of course you know the answer: "We can't do that."

For the next three or four months, we entered the State's Progressive Discipline process.

First, a verbal warning was given and then two or three official write-ups, each one given by a program manager that had never been involved with this type of process.

I attended weekly meetings with 5-8 people [my staff and HR people]. The write-ups defined all of the issues: Tardy attendance, bad attitude toward staff, phone complaints, etc.

The process went through several twists: First, the individual became focused on being on time and staying later, and became more polite to the staff – though follow-through did not improve.

When we did the second write-up I became aware that, while

we were focused on some things that had improved, now we were creating what I could almost not believe: A hostile work environment."

We were hoping that our callers would complain – some staff members asked their contacts to call and give us feedback to use going forward in this process.

After many weeks of soap opera discussions and lots of hours

"Hire the right people, because the cost of not having the right people is very high."

of wasted time discussing this process, I finally came back to my original request: To bridge this person to retirement. Now, after all of this effort, HR agreed and the individual was gone in one week.

The moral to this story has several truths. We treated the individual with dignity and respect, all aspects were handled in the spirit of the Progressive Discipline process.

The process took way more energy and time than it deserved and put both emotional and time-related burdens on many employees.

Having gone through this process, it reinforces the idea:

Hire the right people, because the cost of not having the right people is very high.

As you read the rest of this section, understand that all of the basic management tools, if done correctly, will have incredible positive impact on how a workplace self-patrols and defines the expectations of a high-performance culture.

Let's discuss some of my favorite ways to ensure that dealing with poor performance is effective and owned by the entire organization:

There are no easy answers to the problem of dealing with poor performance.

But there is a simple solution, if you believe that you are managing for the long term and not just to get the next promotion.

All of the suggested behaviors discussed below have an in-depth section in this resource guide. With this topic, I will try to keep to the concept level of discussion. If you are interested, a more more information is available in the respective sections.

In order to have a high-performance, collaborative working environment, you have to start with being able to define a clear and compelling vision that all employees share and are passionate about achieving.

There are three possible types of management functions that your work group is responsible for:

- Operating mode
- Crisis mode
- Initiative/change mode

The first two modes focus on What you are producing and How you produce it. In a crisis, the goal is to stop the crisis and get back to operating. The initiative mode requires more: People executing organizational change need to know and embrace Why.

In the section, The Architecture of Managing People, I frame four basic truths about managing people:

1. People will do what they think they should do, how they think they should do it.

2. You need to know the values of the people you manage, why are they here – you can

be successful and not like the success.

3. The most important thing a manager can do is make sure the team has the same picture of success as you do.

4. As a manager your primary function is to give your people resources and get out of their way.

The primary element of high-performance cultures is a shared passion for a clear vision and shared values.

With these two elements in place, the team will self-manage the poor performers out of the organization.

Once the vision is shared, the next step is to break down the vision, as much as possible, into specific behaviors that are owned by the employees. I have labeled this: A better way to operate.

This involves analyzing the most important employee interactions – clearly defining what has to go right every time, and aligning these behaviors into all of the traditional management tools, including:

- Job descriptions
- Training efforts
- Policy alignment
- Annual reviews
- Rewards strategies

One of my favorite management practices was to annually sit

down with each work group and my direct reports and have employees read their job description out loud.

Once these had been read, I would ask three simple questions:

1. Do you still do what the job description says you do?
2. Are there new things you are doing that should be added to this document?
3. What is in the way of doing your job?

As you can imagine, this practice is very important as jobs change over time, especially when the organization is changing.

More importantly, when the marketing group said that finance was making things difficult, and the finance team said marketing was not following the rules, I had a way forward. I got both teams together in a room, had them read their job descriptions out loud, and informed them that each group had answered the "in your way" question, citing the other group.

I told them that I was leaving the room for 20 minutes, and when I came back I assumed they would tell me how this problem would be solved. I always held the job description meetings six months after last year's reviews.

I strongly recommend trying this out. It empowered the teams to solve their problems, not blame others.

A crucial part of this is creating a reward strategy that focuses on people doing things right.

In today's world, having competitive employee contests will not work. We have all figured out that someone might win, but the rest are all losers. Plus, the Millennials [under 35] don't care about winning – they seek praise.

I had the privilege of watching a training session for the Seattle Police Department police dogs. I asked the officer, "What is the most important method of achieving a high level of trust with the animals?"

I hope the answer surprises you. The officer never punishes the dog. They never want the animal to hesitate. If the dog makes a mistake, they just take a step back and train up again. Think about how much time we spend telling our employees about their problems.

I believe that what you focus on is what you will receive more of. If you are always picking one winner and spending time telling employees what they did poorly, then you will just get more bad decisions:

"What you reward is what you will get more of."

Finally, a conversation about getting feedback from your users/clients/customers. As a manager, this involves receiving feedback from your employees, and taking control of the feedback from your superiors. Take charge of how you get feedback and what you ask for feedback on.

If you have read earlier sections of this guide, you're familiar with the idea that getting feedback helps build the passion of your work group and your superiors.

Defining your own feedback strategy allows you to manage the expectations of everyone around you.

The concept is very easy to do, once you have aligned your vision, job descriptions, reviews, rewards strategy, and policies – you can frame the questions to match your management system.

As an example, the book, *First, Break All the Rules*, identifies 23 questions that the authors attribute to high-performance cultures.

Here are two of them:

1. Do I know what is expected of me at work?

2. At work, do my opinions seem to count?

I spent two semesters teaching a Master's level communications class at Seattle University. At the request of the students, I discussed the class goals – one was the survey I gave out at the end of the quarter on my performance.

I promised that I would bring in real professionals working in many fields of interest, and that we would deal in theory, but that my goal was to also bring a practical element to the class, and so on.

You can imagine how I was scored at the end of the class. Think about what I have covered in this section: vision, job descriptions, aligned behaviors for high-performance production, etc.

Think about what you want your employees to say about your management by defining questions for feedback surveys that you want to score high on. You will be happy you did! What better way for people to become passionate about where they work and who they work for?

The closing thought: Create a culture that empowers employees, by defining clear expectations of how you will manage. Defining clear management behaviors is the best way to manage poor

employee performance. Let your employees manage the poor performance by caring about their culture. .

Personal Growth Through Networking

NETWORKING: The exchange of information or services among individuals, groups or institutions; an interconnected or interrelated chain, group or system.

There are lots of outlets – online and in person – that talk about the power and usefulness of being a great networker.

In its simplest form, getting to know new people, trading information and building your life around meeting interesting people, seems like a no-brainer.

But having said that, I am amazed at how the people that I meet with understand that we should have some time together – but are not really sure of the strategy that might get them the most from that time.

I think networking has changed dramatically over the last 5-10 years. Though I have not been an active networker, from the perspective of "I want to use it for my personal growth," I am

now at a unique place where I need to engage in active networking. I am putting it into practice over the next six months, using networking to build the Loyalty Solutions Group Management Training business.

WHAT PROBLEM AM I SOLVING?

I never try to solve a problem with out first clearly defining the problem:

Over the last 10 years the business world has worked very hard at expense control, and in particular treating human resources as a managed expense, not an organizational asset. This effort has placed frontline managers in situations that they have not been given much training on how to handle.

Additionally, they are being managed by divisional or regional managers who are very focused on the core operating numbers. There is very little focus on building an employee-centric culture.

Finally, the senior management is part of the Baby Boomer generation, who view competition as a core employee motivator.

These frontline managers are in the Millennium generation and have little passion for the concept of winning-at-all-costs.

If I am correct in describing the current problem, in the coming years the solution to this generational divide will be to re-engineer corporate cultures from a competitive-focused work environment to a collaborative-focused work environment.

I am now ready to build a networking strategy to:

- Exchange information or services among individuals, groups or institutions
- Engage interconnected or interrelated individuals or groups of people interested in discussing and sharing solutions to this problem.

CREATIVE BRIEF

WHO IS MY PRIMARY TARGET AUDIENCE?

I am first going to focus on Human Resource professionals who are living in this current employee culture, to verify that I am addressing the right problem. I will also strive to engage CEO-level executives who might be confronted with this issue.

GOAL: To make sure I am realistically defining the issue that I am trying to solve.

WHAT DO I THINK, OR FEEL, THAT MIGHT IMPACT THEIR ATTITUDES AND RECEPTIVENESS?

The nature of the solution to this issue is that businesses need to move their workplace culture toward collaboration – and that is an unknown pathway. I believe that businesses need to discover [the proactive way, or the hard way] that doing the same thing over and over will not get you a different outcome.

WHAT DO I WANT THEM TO BELIEVE ABOUT MY ABILITY?

That I am knowledgeable and experienced in creating highly cooperative working environments that are also very productive, and can handle change better than competitive-focused cultures.

HOW I WOULD LIKE THEM TO RESPOND:

The conversation will focus on understanding their level of interest in this concept, understanding their beliefs about the barriers to acting on this concept, and leaving them with a sense of curiosity about the possibility of this opportunity.

WHY SHOULD THEY CARE?

If my stated problem is correct, they are facing turnover, poor

decision-making, lack of loyalty and passion for the work – and the people in the culture are not having any fun.

HOW WILL I FOLLOW UP ON THESE CONVERSATIONS?

My goal is to find ways to help them with what we discover – the issues they are dealing with. This could be, from my consulting context, an introduction to someone that I think might add value to their efforts, or possibly a published article written by me or others, discussing information that helps bring clarification to their issues.

ANYTHING I SHOULD AVOID?

I will avoid a hardcore sales approach. I want to discuss my conceptual understanding, discover their passions for this concept, uncover which issues they need to solve, and empower them to strategize success.

SOME THOUGHTS ABOUT BEING A GREAT NETWORKER

Adding context to the effort of using networking to build a business and/or a personal social group is, I think, an important component. Here are some collected thoughts that I am using to define the context of my effort:

- To be a great networker, you must be curious. Being curious is, in my way of thinking, the pathway to passion and the antidote

to fear. Going out there to discover whether your problem is real and traveling with the sense of confidence that these networking efforts will be useful for you [but more importantly, for others], requires a high level of curiosity.

- To be a great networker, you must have a clearly defined problem. Remember, never have an answer without a problem. Networking implies that you have something you are curious about. Always define the problem clearly and then apply curiosity.

- To be a great networker, you must be fearless. Rejection is part of life, and having the ability to keep calling and trying when people turn you down can be supported by your personal self-esteem. You must be fearless.

- To be a great networker, you must be prepared. I am using this guide to prepare myself for this effort. I believe that my product is solid, my website is well designed, and my contacts are well targeted. Now, I just need to be confident that I have prepared well and am ready to go – that I am not ahead of myself.

- To be a great networker, you must adapt to the idea that networking is not about them

helping you – it's about you helping them. Your goal is to believe so much in the power of networking, that you are constantly connecting people to other people that you believe will add value to the greater work and conversation.

- To be a great networker, you must be sincere. The idea of sincerity has lots of feelings and emotions attached. I suggest that there are two behaviors that will demonstrate your sincerity: Asking more questions and paraphrasing what you are hearing the other person say. Always demonstrate that you understand key points to the conversation.

- To be a great networker, you must follow up on the conversation, At the baseline, this is a thank you email, but doing a tangible thing like identifying key parts of the conversation, introducing them to a follow-up conversation, or adding thoughts that came to you after you left the conversation, demonstrates the value you placed on the time spent together.

You may think of more ways to use networking as a personal growth strategy, but that will happen because you are driven by curiosity.

In our current world there are no end of ways you can become smarter and wiser – as my favorite beer commercial states, "STAY CURIOUS, MY FRIENDS."

Measuring the Impact of a Collaborative Work Environment

My favorite business truth is: What you measure is what you get. No matter how you got into business, once you are there and challenged with creating a profit or producing a level of production, measuring results becomes the fundamental management tool for success.

In most cases, managers create a dashboard report that gives frequent, reliable information that everyone in the organization becomes accountable for on how the operation is performing.

Having this basic business activity as the indicator of future success, management's role is to create a working environment that supports the behaviors that keep improving the dashboard report.

This is where the conversation about a working culture becomes important: Does a collaborative culture outperform

a competitive culture? There it is: The key dilemma of this section – and, I would suggest – of our current working environments.

> ## As the Baby Boomers leave the workforce, does the concept of best culture change from competition environment to collaboration environment?

This is something that has been studied and written about extensively. I would contend that when Marcus Buckingham and Curt Coffman published the book, *First, Break All the Rules*, based on Gallup research, the overwhelming answer to this dilemma was answered. Collaboration wins in building a sustainable high-performance culture.

My first suggestion is if you have not read this book, either get a copy online or Google the title – there are a lot of open source elements that you can access. I guarantee that it is worth the time and effort.

The way to measure the impact of creating a collaborative work culture should start with having the following two surveys taken. This will give you baseline scores to measure the attitudes about the current work culture. When

you change your managers' ability to understand how a collaborative culture is built, you will have future work culture survey scores, and will be able to map corresponding changes in your dashboard scores. You can view this as your own culture research project.

The first survey is what I adapted from *First, Break All the Rules*. When I was named the CEO of Tully's Coffee, I did exactly what I am suggesting you should do – I had all employees take the survey below.

I separated the surveys by division, but I did not separate by manager as I did not want to put manager competition into the mix. I also held a meeting with all managers to discuss the effort prior to the launching of the survey.

As you read through the survey, be aware there no questions involved that a focused and empathetic manager could not find a way to improve upon, if they wanted to raise their scores.

Also notice how basic these questions are – they are not complicated or hard to understand. But high scores almost guarantee a culture that produces high levels of productivity, improved levels of profitability, employee retention, and improved customer satisfaction.

TULLY'S EMPLOYEE SURVEY

Your manager is defined as the person responsible for conducting your performance review discussion, even if you have been reporting to that person for only a short time. This refers to your current store manager.

For store managers, this refers to your current district manager [or regional operations manager]. If you work in more than one store, please respond to the questions based on your primary store only.

Disagree/Neither/Strongly/Agree

YOUR OVERALL SATISFACTION

1. Considering everything, I enjoy working at Tully's.

YOUR STORE MANAGER AND JOB

2. I know what is expected of me at work.

3. I have the materials and equipment I need to do my work right.

4. At work, I have the opportunity to do what I do best every day.

5. In the last seven days, I have received recognition or praise for doing good work.

6. My manager, or someone at work, seems to care about me as a person.

7. There is someone at work who encourages my development.

8. At work, my opinions seem to count.

9. The mission or purpose of my company makes me feel my job is important.

10. My coworkers are committed to doing quality work.

11. I have a good friend at work.

12. In the last six months, someone at work has talked to me about my progress.

13. This last year, I have had the opportunities at work to learn and grow.

14. We have effective communication within my store.

15. My manager provides coaching and effective feedback on my performance.

16. I am comfortable approaching my manager with my problems or questions.

17. I would not hesitate to recommend Tully's to a friend seeking employment [i.e., when you know someone is looking for a job, you don't hesitate to recommend Tully's].

18. Senior management is open and honest in communication.

19. Senior management communicates a clear picture of the direction Tully's is heading.

20. Overall, how we communicate at Tully's allows me to efficiently do my work.

21. I have the ability to use my vacation and/or holidays on a timely basis.

As you can see from the questions, raising these scores should be a no-brainer...

The second survey I would suggest comes from the section of this guide entitled, Creating a Collaborative Working Environment. This survey is based on the scores of your managers and would be administrated first – prior to any formal training effort – and then once every six months to keep the culture conversation fresh in everyone's mind. These questions are part of the formal collaborative training.

1. IT STARTS WITH CLEAR VISION AND EXPECTATIONS

How sure are you that your employees understand what is expected of them in a variety of situations? Do you believe that everyone on your team understands what success looks like? As a group, is there solidarity of belief for both the vision as well as the plan on how to get there?

Score your confidence 1-10, with 10 being high.

2. UNDERSTANDING HOW TO BUILD TRUST AND SHARED VALUES

What is the level of mutual trust with your team? Do all of your team members share the same values?

Score your team's mutual trust level and shared values 1-10, with 10 being high.

3. THE ART OF MAKING DECISIONS

How well do your team members understand how decisions are made under your leadership? How much input do your team members have in the decision process?

Score your team's trust in your decision process 1-10, with 10 being high.

4. JOB DESCRIPTIONS – A FORGOTTEN ASSET

Do you regularly [at least one time per year] discuss your team members' job descriptions?

Score your effective use of job descriptions in managing your employees 1-10, with 10 being high.

5. THE USE OF REVIEWS

How would you rate your ability to have the review process be viewed as a worthwhile experience for both you and your employees?

Score your team's trust in the annual review process 1-10, with 10 being high.

6. DESIGNING AN EMPLOYEE REWARD SYSTEM

How would you rate your employee reward/recognition efforts?

Score your teams reward/ recognition system 1-10, with 1 being very individual competition and 10 being totally group focused.

7. DEALING WITH POOR PERFORMANCE EMPLOYEES

How comfortable are you handling the poor performing employee?

Score your level of confidence in handling poor performance employees 1-10, with 10 being high.

8. DEALING WITH CONFLICT

How comfortable are you at managing conflict in a way that improves performance?

Score your level of confidence in handling internal conflict 1-10, with 10 being high.

9. MANAGING ORGANIZATIONAL CHANGE

How comfortable are you with organizational change? Do you have a clear understanding as to what you need to do to manage organizational change?

Score your level of confidence in handling organizational change 1-10, with 10 being high.

10. HOW TO BE CREATIVE

How comfortable are you at finding ways to be creative? Do you have a system for fostering your team's creativity?

Score your level of confidence in inspiring you team's creativity 1-10, with 10 being high.

11. BUILDING A SOCIAL ENVIRONMENT

How well do you engage individuals and small groups in conversation that allows for equal exchange of information?

How comfortable are you engaging, considering the time pressures of your workday?

Score your level of comfort with just being socially engaged 1-10, with 10 being very good.

12. HOW TO USE FEEDBACK [INTERNAL AND EXTERNAL]

Does your management style have a feedback component? Is this feedback component a regular part of your behaviors?

Score your level of comfort with having a feedback system and you comfort in receiving the feedback 1-10, with 10 being very comfortable.

13. PERSONAL AND PROFESSIONAL GROWTH THROUGH NETWORKING

How well do you network? Is networking a part of your self-improvement strategy?

Score your level of networking as a consistent personal growth strategy 1-10, with 10 being very high.

14. HOW TO MEASURE PERFORMANCE IN A COLLABORATIVE CULTURE

Do you have a consistent dashboard report that gives a tangible score to measure your team's progress? Does the report have a high level of transparency? Do your employees trust that they can have an impact on its results?

Score your level of consistency at positively using this dashboard report to manage your team 1-10, with 10 being very high.

15. BUILDING A COLLABORATIVE WORKING ENVIRONMENT: YOUR PERSONAL LEADERSHIP/MANAGEMENT SCORE

Add up your scores and look at the level of active behaviors you have adopted in creating a collaborative **working evironment:**

90%=126 80%=112 75%=105 70%= 98 60%= 84 50%=70

Now look at your 5-7 lowest scores and ask yourself: What activities would I like to learn that would have a significant positive impact on improving my team's collaboration and overall productivity?

NEXT STEPS

You now have two surveys that, when used consistently as a progress report for your management team and employees, and in conjunction with your financial/production dashboard reports, will provide the answer to the management dilemma of defining:

> *"What is the best culture for your organization: One built on competition, or one built on collaboration?"*

I started this section with my favorite business/organizational truth:

WHAT YOU MEASURE IS WHAT YOU GET!

What Makes a Great Place to Work

Here are two examples of defining documents, designed to communicate to employees what a great place to work looks like, and how the business organization intends to improve the workplace.

TULLY'S COFFEE CASE STUDY

Objectives:

- Get input from management at Tully's stores
- List all of the policies and activities that a great employer has or does
- Compile a report and assess Tully's status as a great employer

10 AREAS TO HELP TULLY'S BE A GREAT PLACE TO WORK:

1. Business Plan Clarity and Accurate Financial Reporting:

In March, we spent a lot of time discussing Tully's business plan. The quarter ending June 2011 was the first time for quarter reporting in our new P&L format.

Next Steps:

Continued need for improvement in execution of our business plan and much more refinement of our accuracy of financial reporting.

2. Clear Job Descriptions:

Job descriptions have been rewritten for the entire organization.

Next Steps:

Review job descriptions with all store managers to ensure they are accurate and understood.

3. Clear Career Path Progression:

Understand how someone can join Tully's as a barista-in-training and move up through the organization to store manager and district manager or into the corporate office.

Next Steps:

No plan yet. We need to clearly define this progression.

4. Salary Progression:

How should our pay increases work? For our hourly staff, are pay increase milestones after their training period, after working nine months, etc.? When does the wage top out?

For our managers, should salaries relate to store sales volume levels or responsibility levels – for example, if a manager runs a training store – or based upon a manager's years of experience?

Next Steps:

No plan yet. We need to clearly define this progression and how decisions are made.

5. Clarity of our Bonus Program:

We have not yet established a bonus program that clearly connects which operational elements store managers can control toward earning a bonus, either through good planning or great execution.

Next Steps:

We are working to redesign our bonus program. We have not yet figured out how to get accurate information to support areas you can control, such as product waste and COGS business, and some of our revenue plans are not in line with reality. We need your input to complete a quality bonus program.

6. A Clear Review Program:

Prior to April and May 2007, reviews were hit and miss and done on anniversary hire dates. We now have a unified, company-wide approach and have made changes to how you are reviewed, based upon how you perform your job description.

Next Steps:

To have the organization of stores do a mid-year review in early October 2007.

7. Great Benefits:

We completely redesigned our employee benefits and launched the program in May 2007. It is with great appreciation that we increased our overall enrollment by 160 people over 2006, with almost 100% being store managers, assistant managers, and lead baristas.

The company pays 75% and this program is "Best In Class." We now support employees with medical and dental benefits at a minimum of 17.5 hours per week.

Next Steps:

Enroll more employees.

8. A Great Training Program:

Our training program is being completely redesigned with the idea that all of us must become great trainers. In fact, we will only succeed if we become a great training organization. We need not only basic trainings, but great programs for managers, assistant managers, and lead baristas to help support your professional and personal growth.

Next Steps:

We are working to have a complete program by spring 2008.

9. Annual Employee Surveys:

Great organizations listen to their employees. This is demonstrated in both the exercise we are going through now to define a vision and get input, but also in a formal survey program. We launched our first effort in February 2007.

Next Steps:

Resurvey our organization in winter 2008.

10. Legal and Other Issues:

Tully's does business in an environment of ever-changing laws and governmental influence. By going public, Tully's will be required to change some of our policies.

For example, in California, there is a class action lawsuit against Starbucks that our legal team is watching closely. After it is settled, Tully's needs to define how we should all proceed.

Next Steps:

Respond to these changes with as open and clear communication as possible and define the issue so we all own it.

Conclusion:

We stated that we would be giving a 2% cost of living raise to our managers in July 2007. That would be the easy answer, but not the best one. It is my responsibility to look forward and tell you that the issues of a clear career progression, a clear salary progression, and a completed bonus restructuring, and some looming legal decisions need to be taken into consideration and we, together, will make the best decision. This will then allow us to open 20-30 new stores with clarity.

I asked the district managers to discuss this letter and these 10

areas of employment carefully with each of you, so that upon my return, all of us are on the same page as to what we are trying to accomplish, and clear decisions are made with the big picture in mind.

I am proud of all of you and what we have accomplished together in the last 10 months, and eager to celebrate our future successes!

Prepared by John Buller July 25, 2007

THE BON MARCHÉ DEFINITIONS:

Effective Leadership

•   Effective leadership is having a clear vision, pursuing that vision with passion, and remaining focused and consistent. Effective leaders are committed to honest communication, building a strong team, and fostering a caring work environment.

Effective Leadership is...

1. Clearly defining and communicating each individual's role in achieving the vision.

2. Directing and supporting the organization.

3. Measuring and rewarding successful results.

Clear Focus and Execution of Mission and Vision

•   Every employee clearly understands the vision and is

accountable for their role in making it happen.

Clear Focus and Execution of Mission and Vision is...

- Store policies are in line with the vision.
- We invest in assets to support vision.
- Feedback occurs to check vision bottom-up/top-down.
- Success is rewarded.

Quality Associates, All Levels

- Quality exists because we have an organization of people with the requisite skills and attitude to accomplish the vision.

The People...

1. Include a stable core of productive players.
2. Are informed and highly skilled.
3. Are caring, dedicated, hardworking, positively competitive, and have a desire to accomplish the vision.
4. Believe in a reward for performance system.

Quality, Value, Fashion-Right Merchandise

- Quality, value, fashion-right merchandise is the primary reason that our customers shop at The Bon Marché. This selection meets the customers' expectations by providing full assortments of distinctive, fashionable, fresh merchandise at fair prices.

Quality, Value, Fashion-Right Merchandise is...

1. Dominant assortments of premiere, core, and private label resources.
2. In-stock on "NEVER OUT" basics.
3. Competitively priced.
4. Presented in an exciting, friendly, and convenient shopping environment.

Credibility With Associates

- The Bon Marché maintains a consistent relationship with its employees involving open, honest communication, which results in a shared understanding of its vision.

Credibility With Associates is...

1. All policies and procedures are understood and explainable.
2. Our environment respects the dignity of the individual.
3. Management communicates relentlessly on What and Why.
4. The Union becomes our partner.

Credibility With Customers

- Credibility with the customer exists because their experiences with The Bon Marché are perceived to be

fair, consistent, and to live up to the expectations we have created for them.

Credibility With Customers is...

1. Credible associates with a sensitivity to our diverse customer base.

2. Credible marketing demonstrated by our in-stock position on all advertised items, store level price accuracy, and the absence of gimmicks.

3. Stores that declare service expectations to our customers, offer better service than the mass merchants, offer acts of service that often exceed expectations in clean, orderly, and fun to shop [Theatre] environments.

Pride in our Organization

- High esteem is present for each individual employee and The Bon Marché as a whole.

Pride In Our Organization is...

1. High standards of productivity exist [relative to industry].

2. We are known for superior assortments.

3. Groups and people do great things.

4. We have among the highest profitability rates in all of Federated, Inc.

Prepared 1996

About the Author
John K. Buller

Over 40 Years of Leadership Experience

Loyalty Solutions Group, Consulting Founder & Group Discussion Leader
(2010 - present)

Current: Executive Director, 101 Club at Washington Athletic Club (2016)

Recent: CEO, Seattle Police Foundation (2015)

Past Clients: Adjunct Faculty, Seattle University • Seattle Police Department•
King County Sheriffs' 911 Call Center • The Seattle Center
Foundation • Seattle Police Foundation • Goodwill • Center for
Wooden Boats • DA Davidson • Go Net Yourself • Seafair

University of Washington, Seattle, Washington
Lead Public Relations Consultant, Husky Stadium Renovation Project

Seattle Center, Seattle, Washington
Lead Consultant, Digital Communication Network Project

CEO, Tully's Coffee Corporation, Seattle, Washington *$80 million company, 100 Stores, 1,000 employees*

University of Washington, Seattle, Washington - *Department of Development and Alumni Relations*
Associate Vice President, Executive Director, UW Alumni Association (UWAA)
Associate Vice President, Director of Advancement Services

Seattle Community Colleges District, Seattle, Washington
Lead Consultant, Vision 2000

The Bon Marche, Seattle, Washington
(division of Federated Department Stores, Inc., $900 million, 42 stores, 6,200 employees)
Senior Vice President, Sales Promotion, Marketing and Public relations
Director of Training and Internal Communication
Divisional Merchandise Manager

Federated Department Stores, Inc., Seattle, Washington
Lead Executive for the Corporate Marketing Team

Seattle Organizing Committee • 1995 NCAA Final Four
Co-chair and Director for the Seattle Organizing Committee

Creator Owner, General Manager, "Treats Restaurant"

EDUCATION and PROFESSIONAL DEVELOPMENT

University of Washington, MBA, 1971

University of Washington, Business Administration, 1969

UW Intercollegiate Athletics, 1967-1969; Coached 1970-1971

46487876R00099

Made in the USA
San Bernardino, CA
07 March 2017